Apress Business: The Unbiased Source of Business Information

Apress business books provide essential information and practical advice, each written for practitioners by recognized experts. Busy managers and professionals in all areas of the business world—and at all levels of technical sophistication—look to our books for the actionable ideas and tools they need to solve problems, update and enhance their professional skills, make their work lives easier, and capitalize on opportunity.

Whatever the topic on the business spectrum—entrepreneurship, finance, sales, marketing, management, regulation, information technology, among others—Apress has been praised for providing the objective information and unbiased advice you need to excel in your daily work life. Our authors have no axes to grind; they understand they have one job only—to deliver up-to-date, accurate information simply, concisely, and with deep insight that addresses the real needs of our readers.

It is increasingly hard to find information—whether in the news media, on the Internet, and now all too often in books—that is even-handed and has your best interests at heart. We therefore hope that you enjoy this book, which has been carefully crafted to meet our standards of quality and unbiased coverage.

We are always interested in your feedback or ideas for new titles. Perhaps you'd even like to write a book yourself. Whatever the case, reach out to us at editorial@apress.com and an editor will respond swiftly. Incidentally, at the back of this book, you will find a list of useful related titles. Please visit us at www.apress.com to sign up for newsletters and discounts on future purchases.

The Apress Business Team

Advance Praise for *Management vs. Employees*

"*Hayes Drumwright is a world-class entrepreneur. And in this direct, provocative, and honest book, he describes both the path of his life and the route all of us can take to build something big. Along the way, he shows that a leader's ultimate job is not to shield people from risk, but to help them learn and grow.*"

—Daniel H. Pink, *The New York Times* bestselling author of *Drive* and *To Sell Is Human*

"*I believe a person who can turn a negative into a positive can never be defeated–this is brilliantly illustrated in Management vs. Employees. Hayes Drumwright shares his stories of success, and, importantly, failure with a rare rawness that you will be grateful for again and again.*"

—Greg McKeown, *The New York Times* bestselling author of *Essentialism: The Disciplined Pursuit of Less*

"*This is a raw, transparent, and courageous book about the deeper issues that prevent leaders from doing what they really want to do. Hayes takes us on a trip through his own discovery and leaves us with advice and counsel that is practical and challenging. Brace yourself.*"

—Patrick Lencioni, CEO, The Table Group; bestselling author of *The Five Dysfunctions of a Team* and *The Advantage*

MANAGEMENT VS. EMPLOYEES

HOW LEADERS CAN BRIDGE THE POWER GAPS THAT HURT CORPORATE PERFORMANCE

Hayes Drumwright

Apress®

Management vs. Employees: How Leaders Can Bridge the Power Gaps That Hurt Corporate Performance

Hayes Drumwright
Irvine, California
USA

ISBN-13 (pbk): 978-1-4842-1676-7   ISBN-13 (electronic): 978-1-4842-1675-0

DOI 10.1007/978-1-4842-1675-0

Library of Congress Control Number: 2016948742

Managing Director: Welmoed Spahr
Acquisitions Editor: Robert Hutchinson
Developmental Editor: Matthew Moodie
Editorial Board: Steve Anglin, Pramila Balen, Laura Berendson, Aaron Black, Louise Corrigan, Jonathan Gennick, Robert Hutchinson, Celestin Suresh John, Nikhil Karkal, James Markham, Susan McDermott, Matthew Moodie, Natalie Pao, Gwenan Spearing
Coordinating Editor: Rita Fernando
Copy Editor: Kezia Endsley
Compositor: SPi Global
Indexer: SPi Global

Distributed to the book trade worldwide by Springer Science+Business Media New York, 233 Spring Street, 6th Floor, New York, NY 10013. Phone 1-800-SPRINGER, fax (201) 348-4505, e-mail orders-ny@springer-sbm.com, or visit www.springeronline.com. Apress Media, LLC is a California LLC and the sole member (owner) is Springer Science + Business Media Finance Inc (SSBM Finance Inc). SSBM Finance Inc is a Delaware corporation.

For information on translations, please e-mail rights@apress.com, or visit www.apress.com.

Apress and friends of ED books may be purchased in bulk for academic, corporate, or promotional use. eBook versions and licenses are also available for most titles. For more information, reference our Special Bulk Sales–eBook Licensing web page at www.apress.com/bulk-sales.

Any source code or other supplementary materials referenced by the author in this text is available to readers at www.apress.com. For detailed information about how to locate your book's source code, go to www.apress.com/source-code/.

Dedicated to:
Mason
Carter
Trevor
Brinley
Never stop becoming...

Contents

About the Author

Hayes Drumwright has been a serially successful entrepreneur for over 20 years. He has also had his fair share of failure. His innate ability to grow companies organically was proven at Trace3, where he took the company from an idea and $100 of his own money to revenues in excess of $500M. Drumwright is co-founder and CEO of POP, Inc., a SaaS platform that empowers organizations to safely source problems, distribute accountability for solving them, and create buy-in for initiatives in order to scale the business. He is a founding partner in InstantScale, an investment firm focused on early stage startups from Silicon Valley. He is also a founder of one of the top cult Cabernet brands in Napa Valley, Memento Mori Winery. In 2010, Hayes was named the Ernst & Young Entrepreneur of the Year in Orange County and the Desert Regions, California. Drumwright currently serves on the board of Trace3 and POP, Inc. as Chairman, and at Memento Mori as a director and founder. He holds a BS in Business Administration from Boston University.

Acknowledgments

I would like to thank God for never giving me more failure than I could handle. There were times I thought it was too much, but the perspective gained from failing makes us who we are.

While we have reached great heights, I would to apologize to all the people that had to put up with the learning curve I endured over the last 20 years growing different businesses. Hopefully it makes you smile that we could write down the lessons so others could avoid our mistakes.

Thanks to Brian Anderson for pushing me to write this book. It was much much harder than I expected but I am very glad I did it. Your help was invaluable.

Thanks to Chris Laping, Tyler Beecher, Sherri Hammons, Greg McKeown, Adriel Lares, Cybele Tom, Kristin Raza, Sandy Salty, Stacie Atwater, Susana Sipkovich, Chris Bansek, Vicki Wills, my Dad, and everyone else who gave me feedback and edits along the way.

Thanks to the whole POP team for putting up with how much time it took to finish the book.

Lastly, thanks to my family. All of them. I appreciate you all supporting me in all things.

Introduction

There are simple things most businesses must do to survive. Basic blocking and tackling to make strategies, stay profitable, and continue on.

That is not what this book is about. This is specifically a book about how to close the gap between groups of people in order to scale rapidly.

The basic idea for why I wrote the book was actually written down in 2013. I was running a company called Trace3 and I wrote the following story immediately after an offsite with my management team.

"I Wish We Could Do What You Are Doing"

About six years ago I flew out and met with a company that wanted to buy Trace3. At that time, Trace3 was about $40M in sales. The company I was meeting with was almost $300M in sales. I sat down and met with their entire management team that day and looking back, I probably talked too much. I basically laid out my entire business plan to them and they gave me small snippets of their go-to-market strategy. At the time they were mainly just a data storage reseller with a pretty nice service and maintenance arm.

It was clear within the first hour that our companies were vastly different. Not different in lines we sold, different in culture. We were nimble, quick, and embraced new technology and changes in the market. They had a proven model, were a public company, and knew what worked... At the end of the meeting, I had gotten what I wanted. I wanted to know what they were doing wrong and why they had stopped growing. That was in fact the entire reason for my visit. My only regret from that meeting was when the CEO asked me what my plans for the future were I responded, "My plans are to be bigger than your company in five years." That got a good chuckle from his team. I regret it because it was an arrogant thing to say. It is so important to stay humble. I also really liked the CEO and should not have said it because he was having a difficult time growing his company for reasons I was not mature enough to understand yet.

When we walked out to the parking lot, he stopped me and said, "Hayes, I am so impressed with what you and your team have built at Trace3. You are doing so many things the right way. If I were to start over, I would do it exactly like you are doing it. I wish [our company] could do what you are doing." I thanked him, got in my rental car and, as I drove away, I thought to myself what a stupid thing to say. Why the *hell would you ever look at a better business model and not move toward it. Today that company is roughly $400M in sales and Trace3 is $300M. I now understand, running a company this size, why he said what he did. Getting larger organizations to embrace a paradigm shift in the market can be very difficult. As the leader you must explain the "why" over and over and over until you are blue in the face. There must be education and re-alignment. There must be new divisions and additional risk to the business.*

There is even a strong chance you have to cannibalize some of your best revenue streams.

Getting the sales organization to do that can at times almost seem impossible.

I vowed to be a CEO who would never utter the statement, "I wish I could do what you are doing" in reference to a business model. Ignoring a paradigm shift in the business landscape is the fastest way to irrelevance.

Moving forward is hard enough on its own let alone when the employees don't like the leaders.

I set out to write a book that was applicable on both a personal and business level. Some of my favorite books—*Drive, Essentialism, The Advantage,* and *Lean Start Up*—work on both levels.

Because I have a short attention span, my hope is that you will be able to get through the book in one sitting (or plane ride) and immediately have simple ways to apply the ideas covered. I broke the book into four sections to make it simple to navigate. Part I is about how leaders should calibrate their thinking. I titled that "Us." "Them" is the second part and covers the mindset of the people in the trenches working hard to accomplish the plan. It examines how and why they could turn apathetic and entitled. Part III is a methodology to close the gap between the groups. The last part, which was the most fun to write part, narrows in on how and where to start. Consider it a pep talk.

Knowing what needs to be done to become better is not the same as going out and doing it. Having started many companies and having a strong dose of failure in my past, I know starting can be the toughest part of any journey. Sometimes we need a nudge.

Not to sell it short, but the ideas in this book are more common sense than anything else. I don't think I am all that special and when you understand the differences in the way leaders and standard employees think, you will probably come to many of the same conclusions I have as for how to solve them. I hope you enjoy it, find it applicable, and are inspired to start when you finish.

Us

To heal the rift between management and employees, we must look at both sides of the equation. In Part I, I use my failures and successes over the last 20 years as a backdrop to some key questions. Do you operate selfishly or with others in mind to achieve your goals? What kind of foundation have you laid in a personal sense to traverse difficult problems and market setbacks? Whether we lean on mentors, past experiences, or raw guts, we must have the correct personal map to have any chance navigating the "Us vs. Them" issues that are plaguing corporations.

Selfish and Selfless

When I was 12 years old, I decided that I would be a millionaire by the time I was 30.

I was 25 when I started my first real company and was a multi-millionaire by 28.

By the time I turned 29, I was eating ramen and 89-cent cans of Campbell soup for dinner. I had lost the company and was on the verge of personal bankruptcy.

For all of you who have a monetary goal like I did, you might want to rethink that approach. Your goal should not be to *become* a millionaire by a certain age. It should be to *stay* one.

I started a company in 1997 and had grown revenues to over $24M by 1999 but was then a casualty of the dot-com bust in late 2000. Truthfully, it was more a casualty of my lack of strategy, foresight, and planning than any macro economic event. It was in the failure of that company that I lost my entire savings, my wife's savings, and a great deal of my confidence.

We all have events in our lives that send us down a certain path. Mine was when I was 12 years old, shortly after my parents divorced. Financial hardships forced my mother to take a second job as a night nurse in a hospital so she could make rent. She left her four kids alone at night then came home to get us ready for school. She would sleep 3-4 hours a day in the morning. Even at that age, I understood the strain it caused.

© Hayes Drumwright 2017
H. Drumwright, *Management vs. Employees*, DOI 10.1007/978-1-4842-1675-0_1

On Christmas morning of that year, my siblings and I woke up excited to see the presents under the tree. My mom was exhausted because she had worked the night before. She always tried to work holidays because it paid more. I can't imagine how tough it would be to work the ICU ward on Christmas eve, race home at 5 AM to see your kids get up Christmas morning and spend the day with them, only to head back to work the same night. But that is what she did.

In previous years, there had been many presents for us under the tree. This year, there was a single present for all four children. It was a boombox. For me, since I spent many of my weekends at swim meets, I loved it. As I was thinking about the Depeche Mode, Howard Jones, and the other amazing tapes I was going to play on my boombox something happened. Someone was yelling at my mom. My sister was yelling at my mom and wanted to know why we were only getting one present. She didn't even want a boombox. She didn't understand why we had to move and rent a little house. She didn't think anything that was happening was fair. She started yelling and crying on Christmas morning. My mom just stood motionless looking at her with her arms at her side. Then her knees buckled and she collapsed to the floor and started sobbing.

My mom's true goal in life was to be an amazing mother to her children. Her purpose that morning was to make it magical. She was killing herself trying yet even her best efforts weren't working. Boombox and childhood forgotten in that moment, I walked over to her and put my arm around her as she cried.

That hug lasted a long time and it was then I started making plans to become a millionaire.

After years of watching her struggle, I decided I would never let money force me or anyone I cared about to compromise their purpose. I had a paper route at 12, a job the day I turned 16, and coached kids sports in college. At 19, I started a business called Holiday Highlights with my brother putting holiday lights on houses. At the same time, I created a startup selling Christmas trees through schools as fundraisers (because I was too dense to realize wreaths would be so much easier to sell). I was in a hurry to make money. But to be clear, I didn't want to be a millionaire because I wanted things. I wanted money to take care of the people I loved.

I suppose somewhere along the way, in my determination, the last part of that goal fell away. I just wanted to make money. At 25, I started Techfuel, and I knew we had a chance to make a lot of money. The focus was on growth and building wealth. And for a time we did just that.

But a goal to make a lot of money for investors or yourself is not enough to sustain a business through tough times. In fact, that type of focus will have the crew fleeing ship faster than the water comes on to sink it. Which is what happened to Techfuel. That first company had money and profits at the center of focus. The focus was not the employees, the clients, or its partners. It was on money and on myself.

It took me an entire year to get back on my feet after that failure. While completely miserable when in the thick of it, losing everything can be the best learning experience you ever have. When I did finally start to work out what the rules would be for a new startup, I took all of the lessons of that brutal failure with me into the business plan. Your business needs a more important focus than personal gain.

It was in 2002, at the age of 29, when I started Trace3 and truly knew that people are what matter most. The employees of the most successful companies feel extremely relevant to the mission. They feel they have a part in the plan. The feel they can affect the outcome. So I set out with a simple principle as my guidepost: *They Come First.*

This is now something I consider with any new venture. I ask who is the "they" and how do I serve them best. Except for Techfuel, I have founded four companies, each with a different application of "They Come First." I'll describe the first three companies in detail in this chapter, while the fourth is the subject of the rest of the book.

Trace3

Trace3 was founded by me and two other people and we had the mission to create a company that we would want to work for. That may sound trite, but as the company grew from $20M to $100M and then to over $400M, it was something we tested often. When we wrote compensation plans, we thought about it. When we changed something in the organization or with a go-to market strategy, we considered it.

I liked the test of thinking about whether I would work for myself. I am kind of a pain in the ass as an employee. I have extremely high expectations and like to be involved in the strategy. In short, I want to feel relevant. As Trace3 expanded and I had to focus on hiring, I realized when interviewing big hitters that more than anything, they consider leaving the companies they worked for not because of money, but because they craved relevance. Relevance to the strategy, relevance to the growth of the company, and relevance to the brand they were helping to build. This is something founders feel naturally because so much depends on them and their decisions. As we built Trace3 it was key to help everyone understand their relevance and feel like founders. I knew intuitively that when one feels relevant, like a founder would, that one will work 4-5 times harder than an average employee. If I could put my employees first and have them feel this way, maybe my company could outpace the market and we could build something really special.

"They" came first, the employees. They came before me and were considered in all decisions. I made a "Founders" book with the initial 70 employees and we made a second one when we reached 150 employees. Each employee had to submit a pic of their choice, write about themselves in some area of their lives, and finish with how they were relevant to the future of Trace3. At one point, I reprinted all the business cards so that no matter what the job title said, on the back was printed "FOUNDER" in big styled letters. Finally, I started a program called "Defining Your Homerun" where our one-on-one evaluations would not be focused just on past performance, but most of the time focused on what the employees' 2-3 year goals were for themselves. I believed (and still do) that if a leader understands the dreams and goals of the people they lead, they can't help but incorporate aspects of them into the group's goals and activities.

The results of this approach have been impressive. Trace3 was founded with just $100 and is now to over $500 million in total revenue with growth rates over 20% per year. All of Trace3's growth has been funded from client orders. We raised zero dollars and did not leverage any debt. We literally created something from nothing and I expect the company will reach $1B in sales in the next three years.

InstantScale

My second company is called InstantScale. It is an investment vehicle I created to help the best possible companies coming out of Silicon Valley. The concept for InstantScale came about from watching startup companies in Silicon Valley try to take their fledgling products to market with very little sales acumen. Many of these young startups had created truly game-changing products, but struggled to build sales teams and go to market strategies. I looked at the strategy that had worked for me in building Trace3 and applied it to the problem.

The "they" in this venture are the clients, both the Entrepreneur and the Enterprise Executive (think CIO/CTO).

In order to innovate and sustain their company's competitive advantage, executives must incorporate things that allow them to "do more with less" and at the same time increase top and bottom line growth. Most of the great companies coming out of Silicon Valley were very focused on this value prop. I knew there was a need in the market to help connect in a meaningful way the best startups to executives.

We began taking promising entrepreneurs to Silicon Valley to do speed dating with Tier 1 venture capital firms like Greylock and Andreessen Horowitz. After initial success, we expanded the program to include Kliener Perkins, Lightspeed, and many others. We had executives everywhere raving about the access to innovation and entrepreneurs loving the chance to hone and deliver their message to this valuable audience. "They" both loved it.

The Trace3 people at the VC briefings would watch the executives' reactions to the entrepreneur's presentations. When there were a cluster of clients that wanted to move forward with a particular technology, we would partner with the VC firm and invest alongside them in the A, B, or C round of funding. To date, InstantScale has made 14 investments and has a hit rate of over 90% on successful growth.

Memento Mori Winery

My third venture is a love child. In 2007 I was talking with two of my best friends about a project. One of them I met my freshman year of high school and the other I had met on the swim team at Boston University. Our chances of working together in our real jobs were slim because we were in different industries or locations and we were talking about how great it would be if we could figure out how to see more of each other in a way where we could create something special. It turned out we all had a great deal of passion for wine. The problem was we really did not have that much money. Even if we put all our funds together, we would not have enough to buy a winery let alone handle the cost of starting a new brand. As we were talking about how we could pull it off, we had a deeper conversation about *why* we would do it.

We decided that the "they" in "They Come First" would be true wine lovers. Lucky for us, we are included in that group. With this project we got to be a little selfish. Two things mattered most. First, if we were going to make wine, we would make one that we loved no matter what. Quality of the product would be first, second, and third in our decision making process. We selfishly wanted something we could love, share, age, and be proud of. Second, since quality was key, we would not be worried about making money. We would try to break even if possible, but spending time together on the venture and enjoying wine was far more important.

Adriel Lares, who lived in San Francisco, researched Napa to find out whether there was a way to make a very high-end wine without causing the three of us to file for bankruptcy. After two years of research, Adriel found a consultant, a wine maker, and a prestigious farmer to partner with. We named the brand Memento Mori, which in Latin means "remember you will die." This of course was not met with wild applause from the people we ran the name by, but opinions didn't matter much because the name had meaning to us. I had a bout with cancer in college and Adriel had just lost his father to cancer. If the three of us waited until we were well into our 60s, we would likely have enough money and time to build a winery, but after my cancer I have never been confident I would make it to my mid-60s. A name that means "remember your mortality" was perfect for us. We translate it as "Remember to Live."

In 2010, Memento Mori had its first harvest and we have never looked back. It has been a rare business where the one and only criteria for decision making has been quality. In the first years blending process, we used only 5 of the 13 barrels we harvested. We went way over the top with the wood boxes and packaging. We succeeded in making a product that we loved drinking and sharing with our friends. Adam Craun, my friend from college, now runs the brand and our 2012 vintage was featured in *Wine Spectator* as one of the top wines of the vintage, with a 95 pt rating. Almost unintentionally I have learned a great deal of what a maniacal focus on quality can create by watching Memento Mori rise.

They Come First

The three companies I described all follow the principle of "They Come First". None of the companies are about my personal financial gain.

Many of you might tap the brakes at this point and call BS. Rightfully so. It is with a slight smile that I write this next line.

I argue that being selfless can possibly be the most selfish thing we can do if we have a long-term approach to business.

Let's just look at the results:

- **Company #1: Techfuel**
    - Initially strong success and fast growth until macroeconomic downturn and poor strategy forced a shut down.
    - "They" = Profits and personal wealth.
    - Personally close to bankruptcy.
- **Company #2: Trace3**
    - Over $500,000,000 in sales, profitable, 20% YOY growth.
    - "They" = Employees.
    - Platform to launch InstantScale and POP when T3 clients interactions helped to identify gaps in the market and adjacent plays.

- **Company #3: InstantScale**
  - 14 investments made. To date on paper average return per investment of better than 7x.
  - "They" = Entrepreneurs, VCs, and CIO/CTOs.
  - Personal network exploded to include Tier 1 VC contacts and execs in the Fortune 2000, leading to tremendous opportunity.

- **Company #4: Memento Mori**
  - Considered in 2016 to be one of the top Cabs produced in all of Napa Valley. Tied for top lot sold at Premiere Napa Valley ($130K for five cases).
  - "They" = True wine lovers and our friends.
  - Brand awareness due to press and scores has caused massive relevance and demand in the market.

- **Company #5: POP, Inc.**
  - Keep reading.

"They Come First" matters. **By focusing on others, all boats rise. Call it a plan for delayed selfishness if you must; but in truth, your own gain is a byproduct of their success.**

In 2013, when Trace3 was more that $300M, Instantscale was investing in 1-2 companies per year, and the first vintage of Memento Mori was being released to the public, I realized what my true calling was. With total clarity, I saw what was wrong with the way companies manage their employees and I set out to make a platform that could offer a solution. The fifth company is called POP, Inc. The entire platform is based on the principle that "They Come First."

To lay out how to apply this principle, I organized the book in four sections.

- Part I: Us
- Part II: Them
- Part III: Bridges
- Part IV: Leaders Need Followers

My intent is not just to write about leadership. I have read a few books on leadership and often find them difficult to apply to my day-to-day situations. My goal is to relay much of what I have learned from starting and running companies over the last 25 years in an applicable way. Some have failed. Some have done amazing. Every single one has had problems and I truly wish I would have had a book, written by an average person, to lean on and compare notes with. I say average because I sometimes read books by CEOs of huge companies with billions in the bank or founders who are insanely brilliant with 30 patents and I can't relate. I am not them. I had a 3.14GPA in high school. I went to a junior college then to Boston University. As any of my siblings would quickly tell you, I am pretty average in intelligence. To date, I have never worked at a company where there weren't stresses about cash flow.

You don't need to be an entrepreneur for all of this to make sense. You just need to be someone who wants to succeed in making a difference. **You need to be someone who wants to be relevant to the success of the company or group you work for.** And I hope that by the end of the book you will agree that lifting others is the only true path to great success.

Pour a Foundation

"They Come First" is a concept that has led to many successes in my career. But the lessons that needed to occur before I fully embraced the concept were severe. The worst was losing my first company in 2000. That failure was the result of not paying attention to all of the previous experiences that were offering me chances to learn and operate more intelligently.

There are three lessons I used to fuel my growth after that failure. As I share them in this chapter, my hope is that you use them as a chance to reflect on the similar experiences you've had. I encourage you to take notice of opportunities to learn, and more importantly, to apply those lessons in a way that can help others to scale the business. My belief is that if you can do that, you will be helping yourself achieve massive success for all (yourself possibly being the biggest winner).

Dude, That's My Seat

We moved to Alvin, Texas when I was 13. After five years of school in Northern California, I had come to expect certain things. Most of those comforts were completely destroyed my first day of high school in Alvin. I walked into my first class that day early and most all the chairs were available. There was a really cute blonde girl in the back row and I took the chair next to her. I was pretty shy so I didn't say much. About five minutes before class started a boy named Duane came over to me and stood over my desk. The conversation was pretty one side and went like this.

© Hayes Drumwright 2017
H. Drumwright, *Management vs. Employees*, DOI 10.1007/978-1-4842-1675-0_2

Duane said, "Dude, that is my seat."

I replied, "Umm…there are a lot of open seats, man."

"Yeah, but this one you are in right now…that is my seat."

"Ah…are you serious?"

Just then the teacher told everyone to take a seat. Duane smiled at me and said, "I am going to kick your ass right after this class."

I didn't reply but my face went white. I was 5'2" and 100 pounds my freshman year. I had not hit puberty and Duane had on boots, a big belt buckle, and was a lot bigger than me. Needless to say, I was concerned, but being new to the school, I thought maybe it was a joke.

A boy sitting to my right leaned over and whispered, "Dude, you are dead. Duane is a black belt and is going to kick your ass. Sorry man." Turned out this guy's name was Jimmy Dean. Yes, like the sausage.

Then the cute blonde girl touched my arm and I looked at her. She gave me that semi-pained-looking face where you squinch up your cheeks and raise your shoulders as if to say, you probably should have moved.

I immediately realized I was in serious trouble and started sweating from my hairless armpits. Fast forward to one hour after class. Literally before I can make a run for it, half the class had left and was waiting outside. As soon as I walked out of the building they circled around me and Duane entered. He said, "I told you not to sit in my seat and now you are gonna get your ass kicked." I looked at his boots again and started imagining me on the ground getting kicked in the ribs. Somehow, out of some deep "wanting to live" place in my soul, I put my hands up. The crowd quieted down and I said:

"Duane…I am beyond sorry that I sat in your seat. It is my first day here and I had no idea that was your chair. From today forward I will not sit in it again." I took a deep breath hung my shoulders and then continued, "I think everyone standing here knows you can kick my ass." The laughing and murmurs from the crowd spurned me on. "I know you can kick my ass. You know it. And everyone here knows it. How about…How about we all agree you can and just say you did."

Clearly, in the state of Texas, this type of cowardice had not been seen before. Duane looked confused and was quiet for a moment. He responded, "So you know I can kick your ass then?" I nodded. The crowd hushed in hopes he would rush me, but also in total confusion. "And you aren't gonna sit in my seat again?" I nodded again. "Dude, you are a total pussy." And with that he left.

I literally wanted to die. As the crowd cleared, I distinctly remember people laughing at me, a couple shoving me, and then…the blonde girl and two other girls came over to tell me what a jerk Duane was and how they thought I had outsmarted him. I did my best not to cry, thanked them, and started my search for my second class keeping my head down as I walked.

Alvin, being more racially diverse than where I came from, showed me a couple things. On the way to lunch I saw two African American guys throw a white guy in a trashcan. At lunch, I saw a Hispanic girl pull a white girl by her hair across the lunch table and get three good punches in before the circle formed. At that lunch I sat with my sister and her friends and was in total shock.

Later I saw a big football player picking on a little Hispanic kid that had been staring at the football player's girlfriend (who was hot). The football player was laying out some racial slurs and the Hispanic kid, being about 10 inches shorter than the jock, asked him to repeat it. The football player did. He asked him to repeat it again. The football player leaned down so his face was 3-4 inches from the kid's face and then the kid launched himself up with a huge punch, catching the jock in the jaw. Stunned, he stumbled back, and then six other Hispanic kids came off the wall they were standing against and joined the fight. The football player actually did pretty well considering the numbers. I, on the other hand, had never seen anything like this.

All in all, I felt much better by the end of the day that I had made it unscathed. For the rest of the year I never saw another fight. Jimmy Dean picked a fight with me later that year, but by then I was friends with Adriel Lares and I literally think just because Adriel was standing next to me (and he was Hispanic) Jimmy backed off. Alvin turned out to be a good school.

I learned that setting my ego aside and coming at problems from a different angle could keep me out of trouble. This is an important lesson for "Us." When you lead or run teams, people will watch what you do and many times, emulate it. How we handle adversity, bullies, and setbacks matters to those who are watching.

Sword At My Side

My home life that same year was a disaster. The fighting, screaming, and yelling often had me leaving and going to Adriel's house to play video games on his Commodore 64. I still remember winning Ultima 4 and Bard's Tale. His 800 square foot house, on a gravel road in Alvin, became a hideout for me.

My mom was still working a ton, not sleeping much, and we were left on our own a lot. When she was around, we fought and I was constantly grounded. But after being in Alvin for a year I had gotten my legs under me, a few friends, and even a girlfriend. My mom started dating a guy who I thought was a bit of an idiot and they announced we would be moving to a city called Clear Lake approximately 30 minutes away from Alvin.

It was right around my 15th birthday (before my sophomore year) that my siblings and I went for our annual visit to see my dad in California. (After the divorce, he moved to Dallas for a job and then when we moved to Texas he moved to Southern California. We only saw my dad a week or two a year. There were no cell phones, texting, or Skyping back then. We really had very little contact.) He was living in a condo when we came out that summer. It was a totally different environment than what I was used to. It was quiet. There was no yelling. In almost every conversation I learned something. It was weird. Four years had passed and although he had never sincerely apologized for disappearing on us, it appeared he was interested in building a relationship that summer.

When my siblings went back to my mom's new house in Clear Lake, Texas, I decided to stay an extra week in California. I confided in my dad how bad things were at home and how lost I was starting to feel, especially since I was having to move from Alvin to Clear Lake and start over again at a new school. He just listened. A couple of hours later he asked me if I would want to stay with him in California. I looked at the futon he had in his living room that I was sleeping on…thought about leaving my little brother and sister…thought of how totally destroyed my mom would be without me…started crying…and stared at the ceiling all night.

The next morning, I told him I would stay. To date, it is the toughest decision I have ever made and it is also the most selfish decision I have ever made. Without fully understanding it, it was when I decided that if I was ever going to be able to take care of anyone else, I would have to stand up for myself and try to pick a path toward sanity and learning.

I remember the first couple months of school in California having no friends. I taught myself to juggle tennis balls in my room against the wall. I tried learning guitar. I started writing poetry and stories. I was generally bored out of my mind with no friends and no siblings. After giving up on swimming from ages 11-14, I started to take it seriously again which helped. On the weekends when my dad was home, we would go hunting for first edition books and I got the bug for collecting things. I still love collecting books and reading to this day.

During our drives he would talk to me about his turnaround business. He would tell me about the labor disputes he would have with the unions he worked with at the hospitals he turned around. I was interested and he let me start doing the expenses for him and his partner in some early Excel-type program. It was around that time that he and his partner were able to pull a hospital group called Western Medical Centers out of bankruptcy and eventually sell it to Tenet Healthcare. This was a huge event for him, his turnaround firm, and the hospital. He was able to set up a huge foundation in the sale that would serve the community for the next 30 years. Though he never talks about it, I think this is something he takes great satisfaction in. During all this, he got a nicer place and started making investments in the stock market. Life was pretty great.

It wasn't until almost 10 years later that disaster struck for my dad. He did not have to file bankruptcy, but the effects of losing everything again were incredibly painful for him and for those who loved him to watch. I think one of the most difficult parts of it all for me was that I contributed to it. My company Techfuel had raised $6M, of which $700K was my dad's money. Money that disappeared as I lost the company. We were a generation apart, but we had both screwed up massively. In my attempt to help him restore his faith in himself, I wrote him a poem. Here are a few lines:

Sword At My Side

A dream is gone, faster than thought

Gracing our mind with visions caught

Within perspectives solely ours;

Do you think one person can guide his stars?

Or write, on the sky, stories that play

Of victory, hopes, and songs of praise…

You scream, "I'm here, I've soared so far,

But crashed at the last, I'm a fallen star.

Craters have formed and I lost my shield

Just plodding along with workers in fields."

We scream, "STAND UP!!!
Remember your Name,
Remember your Power,
Those you've Inflamed,
Like children whose lives
Are just like your own
And stars burn brightly
For what you have shone.
Give us your hand
We all know your heart
You Will rise again
And make a new start!"

"That moment will come,
We know, but not how;
Make sure you are ready
To see it somehow."

...

"I can't," you cry, "You're all on your own,
I've lost my way and you all are grown,
Gone in directions, I couldn't foresee,
Go find your own lives and please let me be.
I'm not ready just yet, to stand tall again
And be the target of those I thought friends.
I'll be fine just working in fields
With a sword by my side I can't seem to wield.
Its weight is unnatural; it's cold to the touch
I stare at it longing to wield it so much
Knowing a Moment could happen again
When I hold it up high and feel strong again."

This poem has always been very special to me because while I wrote it for him, I think I wrote it for myself too. It flowed out of me from a pure place of hurting when I lost my company. When I handed it to my dad to read he started crying. I started crying too. It was a very tough time. It was another turning point in my life that I needed to learn from. When you lose everything, it is almost impossible to take care of anyone else. It really does feel like you are trying to crawl out of a crater. And watching it happen to someone I loved, not once, but twice, opened my eyes that even smart people can take too much risk.

I realized there is a responsibility the "Us" must have to the "Them." I learned that I could not just think about just myself when so many were depending on me. Not everyone would share my risk tolerance or emotionally handle uncertainty and chaos. When a team is counting on your direction, leadership must accept some responsibility for being a good steward of their futures.

After that, when I chose to step forward and lead, I never again started a venture without seriously considering the downside risk. I starting using words like "Secure" and "Create" in my planning. I stopped always thinking about more for the sake of more and thought more about how to identify risk 2-3 years out and make plans to overcome it. My dad recovered financially and was a huge lifeline for me as I crawled out of my crater. After experiencing that pain, I never wanted to have to "recover" again. I wanted to build; specifically build a solid foundation that could support stories and stories of growth.

Secret Bank Accounts

Once I was mentoring a very talented person named Sandy who was making about $50,000 per year. We were having a sushi lunch and she told me that she was giving approximately $8,000 to her family every year. She did not do this because she had to, she did it because she wanted to. For Sandy her family has always been the "they" in "They Come First". As we talked through it, what became apparent was that in her generosity, she was not saving any money for herself. The money she could have been saving she was giving to her family. She refused to stop giving to her family, which I understood.

The point I wanted her to see, and I hope you see from my stories, is that if you do not take care of yourself, if you do not secure your personal foundation for growth, then the number of people you will be able to help will be few. The number of those putting their faith in you over time will shrink as well.

Sandy and I agreed that we would leave that lunch immediately and go to the bank. It was a different bank than the one she currently used. We walked in and she opened a new account. She agreed she would take the ATM card she received for that account and destroy it. We agreed to the following plan. She knew as she got raises she would be very tempted to give more and more to her family. I asked her to delay that plan for five years. Keep giving them the $8,000 per year every year but stop there. As she received raises, I told her to set up a separate direct deposit for her paychecks that would go to the new bank account. I told her to think of this other account as her "Take Care of my Family Forever" account. I told her we were trying to solve the problem of her losing her income. In her current state, if she lost her job she could no longer help her family. But if over the next five years she put all her extra income (money earned through raises and bonuses), she could secure them for decades. She did it. She developed a formula for how much she would save every raise and how much she would take to build her own assets, all the while giving to her family.

She secured her foundation, enabling her to help anyone she saw fit. She could lose her job and still give to others. She executed a plan to secure her foundation for giving and can now create the future she desires on stable footing.

It is so hard for us to focus on others if we ourselves are in a dire situation. Some can do it regardless, but many of us flawed types need some base level of security. When we fail to secure the foundation for a company or ourselves, we run the risk of riding a pretty turbulent rollercoaster. Most people cannot handle that ride. They might trust you as a leader if it happens once, but if it happens again, expect most followers to get off.

As I explained in the story about me moving out to live with my dad, securing your foundation does not have to be about money. Very often it is about finding a mentor and learning. This could entail leaving a situation where you have plateaued to find an environment to grow. Sometimes building that foundation is about failing and learning from it. It could be the learning earned from higher education. Without regard for money, there should almost always be a learning component. My first day of school at Alvin I learned about self-preservation and laying my ego aside to outsmart someone. I felt humiliated in the moment, but I find myself telling my kids that story. I am now proud of how fast I thought my way out of a bad situation. I learned that thinking beats fighting. (As I got older this grew into a belief that "talking trumps suing".) Look back at the tough moments and ask yourself what you have learned from that experience. And more importantly, did you apply that learning in a way that will allow you to create security and greater opportunity for your future and the future of those you serve?

Grab Your Cape

When my oldest two sons were small, I was looking for something we could do together that they would remember and look back on fondly when they were older. Since there was this thing called "the Internet," driving all over looking for first edition books like I did with my dad didn't really make sense. At 5 and 7 years old, they were probably a little too young to care about that anyway. I was browsing around on Amazon one evening and I found a book called *Master Marvelworks: The Amazing Spider-Man Volume 1*. It was comprised of the original 10 Spider-Man comic books written back in 1962. I decided I would give it a go.

Years later we have read through 14 of these books. This tradition grew into me reading *The Lion, The Witch, and The Wardrobe* and *The Hobbit* (now with my third son included).

I love it. I love it because the heroes in these start as average people. They are absolutely not prepared for what life throws at them. They have to make decisions on a regular basis on whether to run, hide, forgive, love, protect, or watch from afar as people they care about are in danger.

These are the decisions that we, who are nothing more than average people, have to make everyday. I love talking to my kids about this type of stuff after reading. We talk about why the heroes did what they did.

Every now and then my son would say, "Well, the hero really didn't have a choice." That would make me smile. From my son's perspective, when the hero chooses to be a hero, it limits her choices when the time comes to act. I think I would agree with this. I also think it is a fascinating perspective for a kid to have. If one chooses to do great things in life, one must search for paths that lead to great things. They must think about the right thing over the easy thing and consider the good of all over their own well-being. Not easy things to do.

© Hayes Drumwright 2017
H. Drumwright, *Management vs. Employees*, DOI 10.1007/978-1-4842-1675-0_3

Through the remainder of this book I am going to ask you to put on a cape, get uncomfortable, and limit your options to being a hero. The type of hero I am talking about does not have to put themselves in mortal danger or even fight anyone. My version of a hero keeps a broader view and helps others become more than they thought possible. It is a hero who will accept responsibility for growth, learning, and scale. It is someone who accepts the responsibility of leadership in an organization. I believe and this book will make a case that it can and should happen at every level in an organization, whether that be line manager, CEO, or anywhere in between.

Let me give you a real-life example of a normal person doing hero work. Her name is Sherri Hammons and I have been a big fan of hers since the day I met her. I asked her to write a story for me that she lived through that would help me make my point.

Sherri's Story

I accepted my first position as a Chief Technology Officer knowing the software was challenged. The company was a startup in downtown Denver, Colorado, that ran recurring payments for small businesses. (Think, day care centers and gyms.) The CEO had been honest in the interview that there were "issues" with the application. But, my first week was a shocker. The Software as a Service (SaaS) solution had just gone into beta and the company was panicked. The software could run only 300 payments in 24 hours. It needed to run millions every day. At that rate, the company would be out of business in a few months.

I took the first two weeks to observe the technology team and try to understand exactly what was wrong. The technology had been outsourced to a consulting firm in India. There were 19 programmers and a couple of quality assurance people who had been working on the software for more than a year and a half. It was six months late in deploying and now that it was in customers' hands, it was failing miserably. The owner of the consulting firm was on the company's board of directors and very close to the CEO, that same CEO who had just hired me. I knew I had to tread carefully.

During those two weeks, I observed that the code was getting worse, not better. Every day, the technology team would "fix" a number of defects and deploy back into production. However, every day, the number of defects grew. Exponentially. By my second week at the job, the defects had grown from 300 to 800. At that rate, we would be out of business within a month. I interviewed the team to try to figure out where the problems were. I talked to them as a team, individually, and talked to their managing directors. Nothing pinpointed the issue to me other than bad process and bad code. I read the original requirements. They called for way too much functionality to deliver in the original year that had been scoped. Any technology team could only deliver about a third of that. I checked. The team had only delivered a tenth of that, so that couldn't be the problem.

Eventually, I had to admit that the problem was the technology team. They clearly didn't understand the problems they were solving, didn't have the process to be able to react to them, and were actually adding to more and more technical debt every day. I had to change the team. And fast or the company wouldn't be around. But, the owner of that consulting firm was on the Board of Directors. The CEO called him "my brother." And, I was brand new as a CTO; brand new to the company with no credibility.

I set to work trying to figure out how to sell my plan, which consisted of firing the consulting firm, hiring a local team so I could manage and set up the process, and getting the software back on track. Initial conversations with the CEO were met with an incredulous skepticism. I could tell he wondered why the hell he had hired me. So, I went after hard data to show him why I was right and he was wrong. Within the first four weeks of my tenure, I had my information.

I marched into his office with data proving three things:

1. *Customers in the beta program were overwhelming customer support with complaints. The company could not scale and customers were already leaving.*

2. *The technology was getting worse, not better, based on the daily defect rate.*

3. *The 300 transactions per day needed to immediately go to thousands and ultimately millions or the company would go out of business.*

The CEO balked. He yelled. There was no way he could tell his board member he was going to fire his consulting firm. I stood firm. He called people, got advice, and asked me to reconsider. I stood firm. He relented.

By the first month, I had fired the entire technology team to stop adding to the problem, begun recruiting for a new team which eventually consisted of seven developers (down from 19), and I had taken on one of the Board of Directors. My newly hired team began to tackle the enormous technical debt to try to save the company. In the meantime, our company began getting a lot of press. Good press. Within the first three months of my hire, a major deal with American Express began brewing. They wished to white label our offering. Very cool, except that we were having major problems with the technology. We signed them before the end of my fourth month and had to deliver a world-class solution in nine months.

I pulled in my new team and asked them if they could expedite our plans of making the software "manageable" to "exceptional". They stared at me. I bought them alcohol. I promised time off. In the end, I told them:

"You did not sign up for this. You signed up to help improve an existing technology that was broken. That is what I promised. But, the world has changed. We have partnered with American Express. So, we must succeed with our original goals and add to them. By a lot. We will work nights, weekends, holidays. If you want to leave, I will help you find another job. You can stay here until you find that job. But, if you choose to stay, you are all in. All in. And we will succeed. We will make this company successful. We will save this company. And you will have that for the rest of your life."

I sat in my chair and waited. I sweated. I expected them to run out the door. But no one moved. They stared at me. They all stayed. All of them. For the next two years.

Each quarter I had to prove my decision at the Board of Directors meeting, which included the CEO of the consulting firm, who questioned my every move. By the end of the first year, we could run those millions of transactions per day, scale to as large as the business needed, had added two more major financial companies, and met every Service Level Agreement asked of us. That was the best team I have ever worked with.

I like this story because the entire time I was reading it I thought her plan was going to fail and she would get fired. She was completely aware there was a risk. But she decided from the get-go that she was going to do the right thing by the company, even if it meant doing the hard thing. She limited her options by tying the outcome she needed to the success of the company. She had to be brave. If she failed in her mission, the company failed as well. Even though this may seem obvious, there are countless examples of huge companies failing to find a leader when their survival is on the line. Sometimes average people have to find their capes and become heroes.

The Front Line(s)

One of the things that distinguish great leaders from managers is their ability to zero in on doing the work that really moves us forward versus the work we do everyday. Some people, like Sherri illustrates in her story, have an innate skill for it. Some of us want to have our hands in everything and to help every-where. I am in the latter category, but I want to share an experience that got me to think about how to be a more effective leader.

I was working with an executive who was running a startup. To protect the innocent, we will call him Frank. For anyone who has not worked in a startup, the pace is furious and if run correctly, everyone is trying to help everyone else solve their problems and reach success. Frank shared with me during a dinner that he was trying to create an entirely new market space with his company. With so many areas he needed to pay attention to (sales, marketing, product, systems, and finance), he was spreading himself very thin. He trusted two good leaders for two of the five key functions, but he was taking responsibility to lead the rest. In his mind, the most important role he had was to make sure sales stayed on track. He had the original idea for the value prop of the company and could explain it and sell it better than anyone in the company. (This is a very normal founder situation.)

After we had a drink or two, we got to the core of what he was trying to accomplish. He wanted to know what the best way was for him to help his people scale. He felt like no matter what course of action he took he was going to be deserting a group that needed him. He desperately did not want to let them down. For instance, if he spent all his time dialing in the product, sales would suffer. If he went out to raise more money for marketing and headcount, he would be an absentee CEO for a couple months and slow them down.

He compared his problem to being in battle and having the battle be waged on multiple fronts. How could he possibly know which front line he should be on? He did not have the personality to manage from the back tent like some General would do in the movies. He wanted and needed to be on the front lines with his troops. He wanted to lead from the front. We agreed many founders feel this way; but rarely could we be sure about which front to be on when you can't be everywhere at once.

I told him that I once read a book that was operationally focused (couldn't remember the name) and my main takeaway from the book was the way it prescribed handling "bottlenecks." The story was of a factory manager trying to turn around horribly performing factories and what he did was start to look for individual bottlenecks in the manufacturing system. He looked for the biggest one that was slowing everything else down and he would work with the team in the trenches to fix it. That was not a novel idea to anyone; but what the factory manager realized almost immediately upon fixing the bottleneck was that fixing it exposed the next biggest bottleneck. This continued and continued. Even as production began to skyrocket, there was always a chokepoint in the system. We talked about how this applied to his business.

He was running around looking for bottlenecks and trying to fix them with hiring, processes, etc., but his work was never done. Even worse, he didn't feel he was moving fast enough. He thought a CEO's (or any leader for that matters) job was to search for and attack bottlenecks so his teams could perform better, but in a start up it was hard to know where to go.

I asked him what would happen if he stopped. What would happen if he stepped out of the system (or to the center of it) and looked at how to leap the entire company forward instead for push it forward one bottleneck at a time. It was the same advice I had once received from an insanely talented Venture Partner just six months earlier. That advice had changed everything for me.

After some thought he replied, "If I were to step out and do something to leap us forward it would be to write everything down. I would be to write everything down that I had learned from making mistakes, taking wrong turns, and watching clients and employees experiment in implementing our product. If I shared everything we had learned in a book and shared it with employees, partners, and potential clients then I could use it for onboarding, branding, and marketing. If I am honest with myself, it might grow sales faster than anything I am doing today.

What concerns me though, is that it would probably take 2-3 months to get everything down in a way that would be publishable. That would be 2-3 months the company would be left to mostly fend for themselves. That freaks me out."

I loved the idea and at the same time agreed that it would be stressful. Which front line should he be standing on? The one fighting next to his employees in the trenches, or doing something that could MAYBE blast the company forward by publishing something that could reach tens of thousands of people? Work on bottlenecks or try to create pull in the market? My response to this problem was to order another bottle of wine. See, I told you I was useless.

When we left each other, he had not decided, and I was not sure what to tell him, but we both knew a decision had to be made.

In my experience, this story identifies one of the most crippling things about leadership. There are always so many things to do and you almost never have enough information to be sure about your decisions. Because of this, we end up heading down the wrong path a lot. The superhero comparisons in this chapter work pretty well when you have a situation like Sherri did and you can see the clear and present danger. When you can't, odds are that you are going to screw up.

There is only one thing to truly fear about screwing up. Fear it only if you are the kind of person who refuses to admit it.

At Trace3 I started a staffing business. I started a training business too. I started many adjacent businesses that I thought would complement our core business and help the company scale. They didn't. In fact, they were almost confusing to our clients. Some we spun off and some we shut down. Guess who had to eat crow. Me. Turns out crow doesn't taste very good. And once you eat crow a couple times, you will find your team starts to challenge you harder when you come up with crazy ideas. ALL of this will make you want to stop stepping forward as a leader and trying to leap your department, company, or foundation forward.

Don't let it. Not everything is going to work. Put the cape on anyway. *Your true superhero power as a leader is the fact that you are willing to admit you made a mistake AND that you are willing to keep making mistakes. You heard that right. Your superpower is that you admit you screwed up and keep screwing up.*

You will try to never make the same mistake twice, but your willingness to try new approaches to cure bottlenecks and leap your company forward is what will make you truly special.

After three screw ups on new business units at Trace3, I just barely convinced my leadership team to spend most of our profits on a cloud and big data team approximately two years before major revenue could be generated in those verticals. There was a lot of conflict and ribbing about my past failures, but the team trusted that if it wasn't working, we would shut them down. We all agreed that if it did work, we would have a 2-3 year lead on our competitors. It worked and the team agrees now that I am not *always* an idiot, just sometimes.

What surprised me the most was that my willingness in the past to use my superhero powers of admitting publically I had made a mistake and then taking action to correct it is what caused them to actually believe in me going forward. On the surface it seems counterintuitive, but the more I thought about it, it made sense.

It doesn't matter what level you are in your company. Embrace your superpower and grab your cape—you are needed. They need Us.

Them

In order to understand where apathy and entitlement may be coming from in the lower levels of companies, we must look at it from their perspective. Why is communication constantly a problem in corporations no matter the effort spent to improve it? Is there an innate distrust of management and can this be overcome? Why, when we spend millions rolling out initiatives, do they almost always fail to get the desired traction?

What If "They" Don't Like You?

Assuming you have poured your foundation and donned your cape, there are two main hurdles to overcome if you are to move toward success: even if you believe that "they come first," your employees may see it otherwise: as Us vs. Them. Entitlement and apathy are the two attitudes that are the bane of a leader's existence and must be addressed.

If entitlement and apathy are left unchecked, you will find yourself in the situation that is so common in traditional corporate or government structures. In both, there is very often an "Us vs. Them" mentality where management is believed to have an agenda that puts "them" first and "us" last. We will dig deeper into the psychology of this in the next chapter to figure out how to overcome it, but for now let's assume this "Us vs. Them" outlook is a real problem.

Getting Your Arms Around the Us vs. Them Problem

In running Trace3, I had built a firm foundation in the early days of the company when I could touch everyone and influence everything. But at some point, the company began to grow. It was like it went from a toddler into its preteen years. It started to get its own ideas on what worked and didn't work in order to survive. It still gave me lots of hugs and adoration as its parent and it was hard to look on its success without a sense of pride.

© Hayes Drumwright 2017
H. Drumwright, *Management vs. Employees*, DOI 10.1007/978-1-4842-1675-0_4

But then suddenly, I felt like I turned around for just a second and it had magically become a teenager. As CEO, I would stand on stage in front of hundreds of employees and tell them about the brilliant new initiatives we were rolling out. I would wait for my applause, thinking all the effort and thought management had put into the plans, only to see my teenagers in the audience rolling their eyes.

We took pride in the fact that the initiatives would both *create* massive opportunity and *secure* our future as an organization. Instead of the usual enthusiastic applause, I got a sad little golf clap. When I got off stage, everyone told me the speech was great but my intuition was that many either didn't understand the plan or weren't fully behind the changes.

So I did what I think many of us do. I decided I needed to communicate more. A lot more.

I wrote playbooks explaining "why" the new initiatives were important. I started a blog. I did town halls. I did offsites. But just like with any apathetic teenager, talking more or louder was just not getting through to the employees. In fact, it might be having the opposite affect. It took me a while to figure out why.

The company really had not whole-heartedly embraced leadership's plans. It was in no way a full-scale uprising, but change was taking years longer than I thought was necessary.

To repeat—change was taking YEARS longer than it should have. Even with all my secret CEO powers like charisma, stage presence, charts, power points, blogs, playbooks, etc., change initiatives were moving at a snail's pace. As I ventured out, did research, and talked to others I respected, I found that I was not alone in dealing with this problem. To make it worse, we all agreed there was no easy fix.

One of the best conversations I had was with Tom Mendoza. Tom is a mentor of mine on speaking, culture, and growing businesses. He often paraphrases the famous Theodore Roosevelt quote by saying, "People don't care what you know unless they know that you care." When companies or departments are small and the leader can have high touch on each employee, showing you care is easier. With growth, this becomes much more difficult. If you follow Tom's logic you could surmise that CEOs (or any leader for that matter) becomes less and less relevant in their ability to drive change the further away they get from their "perceived" caring about the employees.

As the leadership gets further and further away from the ground level of the business and their decisions are less and less understood by the masses, they become the "them" in the "Us vs. Them" scenario. Any of us can easily conjure up our leaders off in their ivory tower making decisions about the company's future. Rarely does this thought give us feelings of rainbows and unicorns. Mostly we feel dread and angst. Isn't that so telling? How relevant can a CEO be if that is the sentiment in the company?

For a CEO to truly matter, he or she must find a way to connect at all levels of the organization. Otherwise, he will realize no matter how aggressively he rolls out the company agenda (regardless of format) that "People don't care what you know unless they know that you care."

To begin to solve for the problem, a leader must first study where entitlement and apathy stem from.

Tenure, Success, and a Lack of Risk Can Drive Entitlement

When Tom Mendoza was President of NetApp and was in process of endowing the Notre Dame "Mendoza" College of Business, I remember hearing him speak in front of thousands of people on his thoughts on employees with long tenures and how dangerous they could be.

The gist of the talk was that Tom had little care for tenure or previous successes. He thought both could easily lead to the trap of fostering an attitude of entitlement. Since NetApp was named the #1 company on *Fortune*'s 2009 Best Companies to Work for List, Tom knew a thing or two about building an amazing culture and the things leaders needed to be on the lookout for. Tom boldly stated that he expects the most from the people that have been at the company the longest. If they did not share his mindset, there would be a difficult conversation. He believed that everyone needed to prove their worth everyday and those that allowed past achievements to be the measuring stick would be worked out of the business.

I sat listening to this and found it fascinating because after a decade at Trace3 there were those in the business who would be considered "made" or "untouchable" due to their early contributions or previous rolls. Tom argued that if perceptions like this persisted and leadership did not step in to correct it, the following could occur.

As the sense of entitlement grows from the early founders and they become more complacent, they will do things like bully in meetings, manage up instead of down, drive personal agendas versus the company or departments. He went on to say that over time this would cause the most talented people in the company to leave and make recruiting the top talent in the market close to impossible. We know that intuitively everyone wants a chance to be heard, be relevant to the success of the organization, and have a chance to move up. Entitled employees, especially ones in leadership positions, strangle that.

With that backdrop, the tough conversations he would have with early contributors made all the sense in the world. Yesterday's achievements were appreciated and they could both agree you were compensated well for them. Because of that, do not expect them to matter moving forward. The company owes you nothing and you owe us nothing short of your best. If you can give us that, we will attract the best, scale as a team, and create massive opportunity.

Tom's talk really hit home with me. It was simple and powerful.

I worked with people who thought they were untouchable. I worked with people who acted entitled. At the same time, I also got a sense that there were people in my organization who had created massive success and achieved more than they thought possible in their tenure at Trace3. Those people, instead of acting entitled, actually seemed a little lost. It was almost as if they had hit a crossroad in their careers because they never thought they would be that successful. To many in the organization, their lack of clear direction made them seem lazy or apathetic when in fact they just weren't sure what the next big move was.

The following story is an excerpt from a playbook I wrote called "Secure and Create". I wrote it after internalizing Tom's speech and doing a ton of soul searching on what would cause me to feel or act entitled or unsure of which way to go.

> *Earn Your Way[1]*
>
> *Entitlement is like a cancer. If left untreated, it spreads and can ruin an organization. I recently finished an all-day meeting with the top 11 sales people in the company. We discussed many things in the meetings, but one of the main themes we really honed in on was "defining a homerun." It is a topic I used to write about a lot and ended up being a pretty incredible discussion. Here is why:*
>
> *Most all the people in the room had been with the company for more than three years. I started the discussion by asking each and every one of the 11 team leaders to write on the white board their "homerun" when they started at the company.*
>
> *For those unfamiliar with the term, "defining a homerun" is a concept where a team member explains for the group (or leader) exactly what would be their homerun. It might be a certain level of W2 income, quality of life, becoming a VP, helping others succeed, etc. The key is not what it is; it is whether a person can actually articulate it. If an employee cannot define their homerun, then your job as a leader becomes much more difficult. When interviewing people I always ask them to define it for the following reason: If they can tell me what will make them happy (their homerun), then I stand a much better chance of helping them achieve it. If they can't, well, we know how that ends. Now back to our meeting....*

---

[1] http://trace3.com/leadership/earn-your-way/

Each of the 11 people got up and wrote their homeruns when they first started with the company on the whiteboard. We went around the room and each spent 3-5 minutes storytelling. They described who and how they were in their old jobs and why they joined us. They discussed things like quality of life, being associated with an "A" team (brand uplift), making more money, autonomy, and many other things. One of the homeruns was a simple "try and not get fired." That one got a chuckle.

I thanked them and made a new column on the whiteboard. I titled it "Current Homerun". Then I gave them a five minute break and asked them to come back ready to write down and discuss if their homerun had changed during their tenure with the company. Before they walked out, I told them one of the most dangerous things in business is when you hit your homerun. Hitting it can put you at a crossroads in your career.

They rejoined five minutes later and did what I thought they would. They wrote down new homeruns that looked like this: Understand and help my team achieve their homeruns, fully grasp and understand how to build risk back into the team, scale instead of stagnate, become an effective leader, lift others and remove roadblocks for better performance, get back to a player/coach model so I can mentor more, and build a team that offers true value and stands alone in the marketplace.

Pretty powerful stuff. As we talked through each point, concerns came up too. They wanted to avoid doing the same thing day in and day out. Boredom was an issue. They wanted to spend more time with their families. For some, control versus delegation was a difficult topic.

But ALL were VERY worried about entitlement creeping into their teams. You see, many of us took on tremendous risk (career, financial, brand, or time) in order to create this company. Many took great risk in creating their businesses from scratch within this company. We spent a good ten minutes discussing this and how it is true in every single company, not just Trace3. The ones that succeed in taking the risk and overcoming it get the chance to build teams. When they do, the homerun changes.

Many of the early homeruns had a huge dose of "JUST SURVIVE" in them. Many were selfish. Not in a bad way; they were focused on self because before you can truly take care of others, you need to secure your foundation. Years later, with their financial needs being met, they can focus on building teams in order to scale. They can focus on the team's homeruns. It is good to understand most of the individual members of those teams are now just like that leader was 3-5 years before. They have homeruns that are selfish. And that is not only expected, it is good. Helping them secure their futures is part of being a leader. If you do it right, once they are secure, they will pass it on.

The one HUGE difference is these 11 leaders for the most part have hidden the RISK from the team members. Risk they had to endure when they began their journey to their original homerun. They see it as their job to shelter the team from risk and in that mode, they create room for entitlement...

Earning your way in any company means taking on and accepting risk from your leader. When you sit down with your leadership and define your homerun, the immediate next step should be for the two of you to discuss how much risk you are willing to bear to achieve the homerun. If a leader's goal is to shelter her team from risk by bearing all the risk on her shoulders, she will build a team that cannot scale. Notice I did not say a dysfunctional team. It could be quite functional actually. It would just not scale. And we all know how "A" players feel about being on stagnant teams.

As a leader, you want to secure the family and create massive opportunity. Nowhere in that statement does it say all the risk of building a business must be on your shoulders.

Match the risk to the homeruns and help your team earn their own way. Do that well and they will do it for the next generation of team members as they scale. Do it poorly and suffer entitlement and stagnation.

The two key takeaways from this story are this:

- As the leader it is my job to help my best people define new homeruns as they achieve the original ones.

  - Setting new homeruns encourages people to look forward to a plan that has mutual gain for them and the company.

- As a leader, taking care of people is about helping them learn and grow, not sheltering them from risk.

  - Generous people can accidently cause entitlement by shouldering risk.

A Lack of Understanding Drives Apathy

You can try to hold off the apathy for as long as you can, but eventually something happens in the lifecycle of most every company. There will come a point in time where "leadership" will have to make very hard, uncomfortable choices. The only guarantee when this occurs is that not everyone is going to understand why the choice was made and the "Us vs. Them" chasm will grow. It's probably important to note here that there will be no "silver bullets" to solve for every potential problem that will arise but the relentless pursuit of eliminating apathy will go a long way to ensure maximum success.

Instead of focusing on simple examples that cause apathy like layoffs, no bonuses, acquisitions, etc., let's look at an example of something you would think would make people happy but backfires.

For instance, let's say that you have a VP spot open up on your staff because the company is growing so fast. Your success and personnel growth has caused you to form a Business Development department. You believe that you would like to promote from within because you feel it is not only good for the culture, but also because you feel it helps with momentum. So you and your team come up with three finalists for the promotion and begin the evaluation process.

These are exciting times as all three candidates have been with the company for years. They have teams that they have built and you know would be excited to see their leader picked for the promotion. Before you make the decision on whom to promote, you have a board meeting and a board member puts a terrific outside candidate in front of you for the job. You have a phone call with the outside candidate and like her, but are not sure you have the time to bring her up to speed/train her since the company is moving so quickly. You have a couple other people on the team meet with her and word gets out that you are looking outside the company to fill the position. The rumor bothers you since you were leaning internal, but you wait to hear back from your team on their thoughts.

After two weeks you make the decision to go with an internal candidate. You tell the internal candidates they were exceptional and there will be more opportunity in the future. That being said, you are moving forward in promoting their peer for the job. They handle it graciously, you small talk a bit, and they leave your office.

At the town hall that week you get on stage in front of the teams and have the new VP of Business Development come up and talk about his plans. As you stand on the side of the stage and listen to your newly minted leader speak, you scan the crowd to see how the message is being received. While many are paying attention, you notice the two candidates you did not pick for the job sitting next to each other. One is checking her phone and the other whispers to her then gets up and walks out. You also notice some of the people on their teams are shaking their heads. This gives you a moment of pause but you refocus on you new VP's speech and are happy with the applause at the end of the talk.

So what happened here? Let's look at what you know:

- You are the leader of a successful company that is growing quickly and creating opportunity for many.

- You gave three people who were happy in their jobs a great opportunity to grow.

- You picked only one of them.

- You also let the entire company know you would consider looking outside the company for talent at the executive level.

From these simple moves, which almost every company makes, different scenarios can develop.

Best case scenario: The two people you did not pick for the job are open and honest with you about being disappointed they were passed over but understand and everyone gets back to work. When the new VP of Business Development rolls out initiatives, they, along with all the other leaders, do everything they can to support their success.

Mid case scenario: The two people you did not pick are disgruntled. They are not just bummed you didn't pick them, they know competition will be worse in the future because you are considering outside candidates. Since they are stand-up people, instead of staying somewhere they are disgruntled, they quit to find something else.

Worst case scenario: The two people don't understand why they didn't get the job and after the process are a bit disillusioned about their upside in the organization and are apathetic toward the company…and they stay. When in leadership type meetings, they put on a happy face. As soon as they leave the meeting, they go to their closest five peers and bitch about management.

Yes, I am saying it would be a better scenario if they quit. Having apathetic people stay with the organization and stand around the water cooler poisoning the well can destroy a once great culture. It also makes it very hard for management to understand why initiatives are not getting traction because disgruntled people will nod yes to new initiative launches when sitting in the conference room then leave and tell their teams not to engage.

I like that example because it is counterintuitive. You as a leader are trying to do something good—promote someone—and it twists its way into being a potential negative for those who get passed over. Fast growth has a great deal of accidental carnage like this.

Another common example of good intentions gone astray could be like entering an adjacent market due to solid market research but then the product fails to get traction as expected. While the employees might applaud the bravery at first, as the move continues to pull funding away from the core business, apathy in the core will grow.

I could name hundreds of tough choices executives have to make, but the point is this—**when your company hits that point where you have to make a really tough call, there is only one guarantee. That guarantee is not everyone in the organization will understand it let alone agree with it.** And it is in that very moment that it begins. That is when the "Us vs. Them" divide in organizations plants its seeds. Management makes a tough call and your loving, hugging pre-teen company starts finding some teenagers hanging out by the water cooler. Those teenagers could be people in the trenches or just as likely people in the executive staff. Apathy can creep in at any level. When it finds roots, things get much more difficult. If it grows legs, it makes change and initiative very difficult to execute.

People Don't Care What You Know Unless They Know That You Care

As a leader, when you are constantly battling internally in your company, it is hard to get to the truth of where the biggest pain points around change are.

It took my stepping down to get a good sense of what was going on at Trace3. The masses didn't trust that management had their best interest at heart when they were making changes and no amount of overcommunication was going to change that. Without trust as a centerpiece, exerting my will and reasoning was going to fall on deaf ears.

To use an analogy, change involves giving up the "bird in hand" and moving to something riskier/unknown. Most people just like to sit and pet the bird rather than change. As the bird ages and flies shorter and shorter distances, they talk to it, care for it, and love it. Do you tell them, in a louder and louder voice, that the bird in hand cannot sustain them forever, that they will have to evolve or die? Well, that is not going to resonate for many of them till they see that bird disintegrate right in front of them and it leaves them holding nothing.

How often in life do you listen to someone's advice in moving from something that is working for you to a riskier plan?

How much does it decrease your odds of taking that advice if you don't like or don't believe in the person advising you?

Lastly, even if you do like the person *and* believe in them, how do you know they care about you and your future the same way that you do? How do you know they have your best interest at heart? I mean, in corporate examples, didn't leadership just make two moves up in their ivory tower that made absolutely no sense to you and hurt people you cared about? Couldn't that easily happen to you? Why should you trust their plans for the future?

When I stepped down, people were less afraid to tell me what they thought. More importantly, they were less afraid to tell me what they were confused about and what was causing apathy in a company they really wanted to believe in. I learned something in those conversations.

Leaders, real leaders, can be valuable. But giving a true voice to your employees, I mean *really hearing them,* will attack apathy at its roots and scale your business faster than any charismatic leader could. Bi-directional safe communication channels are needed instead of more of the same old top-down communication methods.

"They" are already overloaded with people telling them what to do. If you want employees to opt in and engage with change initiatives, leaders need to understand their people's homeruns and the employees need answers about the things they don't understand.

After running Trace3 for 12 years I had suffered plenty of war wounds battling these culture killers. I came to the conclusion that building a company to attack the "Us vs. Them" problem was the way I could create the most value in the market as well as do something I find truly fulfilling. To focus on it full-time, I decided in 2013 to step down as CEO.

We have spent the past two years creating a platform to make adoption for change as simple as possible. So far, the journey has been incredible. Before we get to deep into driving out apathy in an organization, we must first briefly focus on whether leadership has any real credibility to be trusted.

Stop Wasting Money On New Initiatives

Trace3 had just grown from $110M to $186M in one year. From the outside, we looked like a wildly successful company. The problem was that if you walked into an executive meeting, it felt a bit like a Kardashian reality show. I would get on a whiteboard and pontificate, a few brave souls would disagree with me, and when they did I would very often end up talking over them and getting my way. There was fighting, but it wasn't healthy. To compensate for how overbearing I was, there were cliques formed and people were having "meetings after the meeting" to vent their frustration to each other. Sadly, there was very little honest communication.

It was during this time a person on the team handed me a book called *The Advantage* written by Patrick Lencioni. You may have heard of other books he has written, such as *5 Dysfunctions of a Team* and *Getting Naked*. Little did I know that reading *The Advantage* would end up changing the course of my career.

© Hayes Drumwright 2017
H. Drumwright, *Management vs. Employees*, DOI 10.1007/978-1-4842-1675-0_5

I remember being on an anniversary trip with my wife when I finally picked up the book. She was 9 months pregnant with our fourth child and we were relaxing by the hotel pool. She asked me what the book was about and I started laughing. I told her it was a management book about how to build teams, achieve goals, and drive your company's culture. She looked at me funny with this response since for years I had been telling her that was what I excelled at. I started reading and she quickly fell asleep. She woke up a little over an hour later and saw me sitting in my chair with my head in my hands. When she asked what was wrong I blurted out that I had been doing everything wrong. She had the nerve to start laughing at me in my moment of despair. This of course made me start laughing, but I was serious. I told her that after reading just 80 pages I knew I was screwing everything up. She said if I had grown a company from zero to over $180M I couldn't be doing *everything* wrong, then promptly fell back asleep.

She knew how fast the company had been growing, but had little insight into the real struggles I was having in getting the company to change. Many of the new initiatives I was running were falling flat. The executives would agree with me in the conference room and then, for some reason, I could not get to the bottom of why they would fall flat and not get traction. This was beyond frustrating, because I spent most of my time as a leader trying to explain "why" the changes were necessary and even with management saying they agreed with the plan, we just couldn't execute at a material level.

Still sitting by the pool, I picked up my cell phone and called my admin. I was only a quarter of the way through the book, but it was clear as day to me that I needed help. Patrick Lencioni (the author) had a consulting firm that could deliver a two-day offsite conference to instruct your management team on the philosophies explained in the book. It is the single most important thing I have done so far in my career. The amount I learned in just two days about the strengths and weaknesses of my leadership style was astounding.

After that offsite, Trace3 went from $186M to $300M in one year. We literally skipped the $200Ms. Here are a few of the stories that helped us change.

The Mix of Personalities Matters Much More Than You Think

One of the more fascinating things I have learned in business was from a story I was told at that offsite. The story they told us was as follows:

There was a simulator test being run on a top group of astronauts. The simulation was a rocket crashing into the moon. They gave each of the astronauts a personality test. They used the well-known Myers-Briggs test. For the first test, they grouped all the astronauts with strong "strategic" personalities together and put them in the simulator. The team had to work together and figure out how to keep from crashing. The strategic-minded team worked together beautifully. There was no screaming or fighting. They brainstormed ideas, pontificated, tried everything they could think of and...crashed 100% of the time.

They then decided to test the other side of the spectrum. They put in a "tactically" minded group of astronauts in the simulator. They operated with a different mindset. They were detailed and thorough. They made lists and went down each item checking off possible options. Once again, the team of like-minded individuals got along tremendously well. There was little tension or shouting as they too...crashed 100% of the time.

The next test used a sampling of each group. There were both tactical and strategic minds on the team. Here is what happened.

*They fought. **They fought a lot.** Certain team members got to the point of coming to blows over how to avoid crashing.*

But through all that conflict a funny thing happened. Since they came at problems from different perspectives and found a way to hear each other, they were able to make progress. They might not have liked each other during the process but they succeeded in avoiding crashing into the moon over 60% of the time.

The point is that in order to make real progress, there needed to be conflict. Like-minded people don't challenge each other enough and agree too easily. When you are dealing with serious issues, conflict and debate is a necessity. There were other supporting stories and examples of why conflict is necessary and if you would like more detail on it I encourage you to read *The Advantage*.

We discussed how conflict, like anything, falls on a spectrum. There is straight up conflict avoidance (where no one says much of anything) on one side of the spectrum. All the way to the other side is totally unhealthy conflict where people are choking each other and coming to blows. Neither end of the spectrum is what you are shooting for as a leader of a team. Your goal is to end up somewhere in the middle. They call that *healthy conflict*. Team members are able to speak their minds, be heard, and debate crucial issues. And they are able to do this without taking other team members opinions personally. This last part is the tough part. In order to understand how to accomplish this, we were asked to have each person on our team to take a personality test. We then spent a small amount of time understanding each person's type and what the strengths and weaknesses of the type were. I had done this many times before, so at this point in the offsite I was concerned I wasn't going to learn much. It wasn't until the astronaut story was combined with teaching us about *attribution error* that we all started to have epiphanies about how to have healthy conflict.

Attribution Error

According to Lencioni, *fundamental attribution error* is as follows: We human beings tend to falsely attribute the negative behavior of others to their character, while we attribute our own negative behaviors to our environment. In other words, we like to believe that we do bad things because of the situations we are in, but somehow we assume that others do bad things because they are predisposed to being bad.*

(*As explained in Patrick Lencioni's *Field Manual for Overcoming the Five Dysfunctions of a Team*.)

You have to kind of love this. We always give ourselves the benefit of the doubt but we so rarely do that to others who disagree with us. We not only think those who disagree with us are doing it to upset us, but that they are probably doing it on purpose too. When we let our minds apply these negative characteristics to other team members, that is when we reach the unhealthy part of the conflict spectrum. Getting to know your team's personality profiles, understanding their backgrounds, and taking a moment to give their opinions some non-emotional critical consideration will keep you in the healthy conflict zone. Teams that can achieve this have a chance for real debate, iteration on ideas, and progress.

So it is one thing to conceptually understand these truisms. It is another to put it in practice. After hearing this astronaut story and all about attribution error at our leadership offsite, I realized how many mistakes I was making as CEO. I was hiring very smart people, but I was not making sure there was a mix of personalities that would challenge each other. I was doing very little to make sure there was conflict let alone healthy conflict. I also had a tendency, as many of you may have, to be overbearing when I thought I had a good idea. I would shut down healthy debate and argue until the team folded and saw things my way. I hope that none of this sounds familiar to you and you have no problem staying quiet as one of your ideas gets beat up by the team. This is something I still work on.

So hopefully these concepts make sense when applied to a small direct team. Let's look at them when applied to the larger organization. I would like to make an argument that, in most larger corporations (let's say over 1,000 employees), there is a high rate of attribution error. As I stated in the previous chapter, eventually in a company's lifecycle, management will have to make decisions that not everyone understands let alone agrees with. This will cause employees to apathetically gather around the water cooler and discuss what is going on. There is a rather common conclusion that the masses will reach. I am calling it *corporate attribution error*.

Corporate Attribution Error

Corporate Attribution Error (CAE): Employees have a natural tendency to believe that management has a blatant disregard for the well-being of employees. In fact, most corporations are making decisions to grow and scale in order to create more opportunity for current and new employees.

In interviewing many turnaround CEOs, there are a couple themes that stay constant. First, the good turnaround guys understand that most all the answers about what is wrong with the company and what needs to be fixed can almost always be found with the employees. Second, when they get enough information to make decisions and cut a large part of the staff, they are doing it to save jobs. You will read a headline like "New CEO Cuts 40% of Staff of Struggling Company." If the new CEO who was brought in to save the company could write the headline it would read, "New CEO Makes Move to Save 60% of the Jobs." If the new CEO fails in the turnaround, 100% of the jobs are gone. Isn't that worse than losing 40%?

And it is in these very tough situations where corporate attribution error grows. Most all decisions made at the top are to create more opportunity, become more competitive, or maybe just triage horrible moves made in the past. When the masses don't understand, it will cause apathy.

So I know…you are now probably wondering why I called this chapter "Stop Wasting Money on New Initiatives". Well just think of what corporate attribution error does to a new initiative!

Most companies are wasting money on new initiatives because most new initiatives fail to get real traction! In fact, Gallup states that 70% of all change initiatives in corporations fail. 70%!!! And if you think about it, isn't a new initiative by definition a change initiative? You are starting a new initiative in order to add, improve, or change something. All three of those are change, which means 70% of all initiatives fail. Brutal.

The root cause of failure for initiatives is not about how functional or dysfunctional the leadership team is. Most management teams are smart and have good intentions. Some have even gone to offsites like I did to make sure they can build cohesive teams that have healthy conflict.

Entitlement, apathy, and corporate attribution error are the root cause of initiative failures in corporations. If you cannot solve these problems with your employees, moving your company forward will be incredibly difficult.

A normal response to try to solve these issues is to make changes at the top or cuts in middle management to show how you will not stand for these new initiatives failing to get traction. But the new leaders will not be able to drive the initiatives to success either. Again, employees, will not normally go out of their way to change for people they don't like, respect, or think have their best interest at heart. Throw on top of that the general sentiment that corporations look out for themselves first and are not trying to create a better future for their employees and you have a real problem.

Until you can solve for the root cause and overcome entitlement, apathy, and CAE, I would stop wasting money on new initiatives.

Barfing Downhill

So how do we as leaders try and fight this corporate attribution error? I can tell you what most of us do. We communicate more. So many times in management we stand on stage and barf our plans down onto the audience, never taking into account the fact that if they think we don't care about them, they probably aren't listening. In fact, with the hundreds of companies I have worked with over the years, communication is always at the top of the list on feedback surveys of things the corporation needs to do better. So we schedule an all-hands meeting or Webex to fix it. We tour around the globe or country and hold town hall meetings. If things are going well we might even have a company offsite with main stage presentations and departmental breakouts. In these presentations we will touch on strategy, mission statements, initiatives, metrics, etc. We will probably also spend a lot of time explaining to the teams "why" we need to do what it is we need to do. We hope that if we can get the why across effectively, they will get on board and help with the "how".

We have this hope (desperate need?) to be understood. We feel at the top if the masses could understand why we are doing what we are doing they would surely back it. This is what we tell ourselves. And in a healthy organization, this is many times true. But what if there is a great deal of apathy in the company? How well does a well presented "why" do in those situations?

Take a look at the chart in Figure 6-1.

© Hayes Drumwright 2017
H. Drumwright, *Management vs. Employees*, DOI 10.1007/978-1-4842-1675-0_6

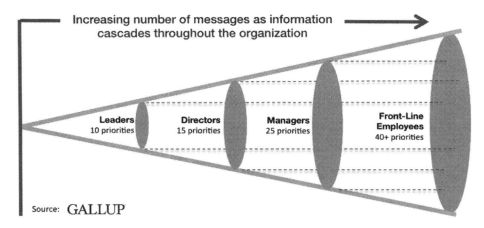

Figure 6-1. The message cascade in typical organizations

When you take a look at this chart, you start to realize what your people are up against. At the top of the food chain in leadership, it seems simple—if we can accomplish these 10 initiatives, the company will be on track for growth and scale. But by the time your message reaches the trenches, what chance do the front-line employees have of making anyone happy? They have to make some tough choices. There is only so much time in the day and only so many masters they can serve.

Look at the way the arrow is pointing on the chart. The communication is flowing in one direction. This is a major issue. Even when you hold town halls, the unfortunate truth is that people are very hesitant to ask the really tough questions in those meetings, for fear of repercussion. The people who do speak are often vocal, but rarely represent the common voice in the room. But even if their questions did have the backing of the entire room, how are you as a fly-in leader supposed to know that?

I watched something happen to a client of mine that might help illustrate this dilemma. We will call this executive Jack.

Jack ran a mid-sized business and prided himself on being in tune with the needs of his employees. He was just kicking off his management offsite with his team of seven leaders who reported directly to him. It was a good group that had gelled over the years of working together and was comfortable with conflict. The VP of Engineering walked into the conference room with a huge stack of papers. He announced that it was the results of the engagement survey that HR had just run. There was a soft groan from the group followed by a chuckle from Jack. It always took them hours to go through engagement survey results, but Jack knew the content was worth it.

Fast-forward eight hours and the debate around the key issues from the employees' perspectives was coming to a close. It was not super easy to decipher, but it appeared in the 200 pages of open answers in the engagement survey that the engineers in the company were very concerned about their career paths. There were comments like:

"The market is moving quickly and management is forming teams around new technology, but I didn't make that team. What does that mean for my future?"

"There seems to be a lot of attention on new skills but my job is crucial to the success of the business. I do not have time to learn new skills. What does this mean for my future?"

Jack decided to try to do something cool. To try to address this fear and uncertainty around the engineering team's need for career path clarity, they created an initiative called "Rise of the Engineer!" Jack told the leadership team he thought the engineers would love the name because it had that *Terminator* kind of feel to it. He assigned two of his leaders to come up with the details on how they would address the issues and roll out the plan.

Over a month later, Rise of the Engineer (ROE) had been iterated on a few times and was ready for launch at the company all-hands meeting. The company was going to spend approx. $3,000,000 rolling out the program that would teach a core curriculum of soft skills and new tech in both cloud and big data, while also giving the engineers "electives" they could take to follow their interests (aligned to company need).

Jack approved the plan after his two leaders presented it to him and had informed him they had tested it with a handful of the engineering leaders whom seemed very receptive and happy the team was finally being heard.

On the day of the all-hands meeting, the engineering leader who helped create the initiative got on stage and started to explain it to the engineering team assembled before him. Jack was not present in the room as he was speaking to the sales team about their goals during that time.

Before Jack could finish his presentation, a few of his direct reports were moving over to the side of the stage. He wrapped up, took a few questions, and then moved offstage to find out what was going on. He was quickly informed that the engineers were angry and Rise of the Engineers was getting ripped apart in the other room. Jack, never quick to overreact, joked with them, "How could they not like it after we gave it such a great name?!" No one laughed. "Fine, let's see what is going on."

The engineers were filing out of the room as Jack entered. His VP of Engineering was having an animated conversation with his co-architect for ROE. The VP of Engineering had been with the company for a long time but was new in the role. He immediately admitted he did not do that well on stage. As he started rolling out the initiative, he got nervous, fumbled a few of the details, and the audience starting asking some tough questions before he could finish. The toughest came from one of the longest tenured employees. He asked, "How exactly do you expect us to do all this training when we are already 100% utilized? What do you think the reps in the field will say about us being out for four days of training? And who picked the curriculum? It was clearly someone who does not deal with clients day to day." The VP had answered the questions as best he could and kept presenting the features of the program while getting peppered with questions.

As Jack listened, he began to get frustrated. In order to be a company that could deliver in the future, he had to keep the skills of his people ahead of the market. He knew that. What frustrated him is that he was trying to create an initiative for the team that he thought they had *specifically* asked for in the engagement survey. He sure as hell was not going to waste $3,000,000 on something they wouldn't even use.

As Jack and the team calmed down, they decided that the 4-5 people that spoke up at the all-hands might not be a representative of the hundreds of people in the group so they rolled out a reined back version of ROE. Participation was minimal. It was super hard for Jack to figure out why. He knew with the experience his VP had had on stage his VP might not be promoting the program as much as necessary to get buy in; but it could also be the questions and concerns from the 4-5 people who spoke up were legitimate.

As I was spending time commiserating with Jack over a drink about how complicated these types of issues were for leaders to work through, I told him about something I was working on.

At the time I had spent 3-4 months building a prototype of a crowdsourcing platform that I was calling "Portal of Pain." The name always got laughs but at the time I was trying to name it for what I wanted it to do. The concept was I would have an anonymous platform where employees could tell me their issues. I could use it to skip level manage, get feedback on problems we were trying to overcome, etc. Jack thought we should give it a try and see what happened.

Jack and his VP came up with the following question to ask the entire engineering team at his company:

"It is clear the methods management used in creating ROE were not up to your expectations. We want to deliver program that not only keeps our teams competitive but ahead of the curve. Please log into this Portal of Pain event and tell us what needs to be in ROE for you to engage with the initiative and make it a huge success. All of your responses will be anonymous and you will be able to see and vote (like or dislike) on your peer's entries. The most liked ideas will rise in the app and I, as your CEO, will pick the best ideas to incorporate into an ROE program created with your feedback. The Portal of Pain event will last for 72 hours only and then close forever. Please log in and give your honest feedback so we can make ROE a huge success."

What happened after that was super interesting. First, almost 70% of the engineering organization logged in. Second, as people logged in and began voting on each other's ideas, a "common voice" was identified. Jack was able to see which ideas/ROE features had the most votes because they rose to the top of the scoreboard. Instead of taking hours going through an engagement survey, in seconds he could see where the masses felt he should be focusing to solve their problem. Next, in addition to idea entry and voting, employees could comment on each other's ideas. Sometimes small arguments even broke out. Even if an idea did not get a ton of "likes" and rise to the top, if it had 30 comments it was something that was valuable for him and the VP of Engineering to see where big debates were happening so they could address them. These were the more obvious benefits of using the Portal of Pain. The most intriguing discovery was something less obvious.

Of the feedback that came in through the tool on how to roll out the ROE initiative, roughly 75% of it was not new. **75% of the feedback for what the engineers wanted in ROE was already in the program! It had already been presented to all of them on stage as features of the program, yet they entered it into the session and much of it got voted to the top as if they had never heard it before.** This was cause for another drink.

Jack and I discussed how this could possibly be happening. Even worse was I had run a couple of my own sessions after town halls to double-check people were understanding the message I was trying to deliver and I was seeing similar results. People were not hearing what I was saying, they were confused by it, or they needed it said a different way. As we tried to get to the root cause of the problem, Jack said something that has really stuck with me.

He said, "Ya know Hayes, at this point it really doesn't matter why they didn't hear us when we were on stage. What matters is that if I act on their feedback from the session now ROE is *their* idea. It is their initiative, not management's. We will add the extra features that we can afford and make sense and I am going to reroll it out. I will give them credit for all of it and see if participation changes."

Within one week of the Portal of Pain session closing Jack laid out the plans for the new improved ROE incorporating the team's ideas around time, equipment, curriculum, and structure to the engineers. Within nine months, 80% of the engineers had completed the curriculum to better their career path and kept the company successful. It was nothing short of a wild success.

As Jack dug deeper into why they did not hear all the features of the program the day it was rolled out, what he learned was that his VP had said a couple things in the beginning— assumptions he had made really—that the masses in the audience didn't agree with. Due to this, the audience started to tune him out. It was Jack's belief that this often happens to speakers on stage without their knowledge. They are speaking and going through a program, never realizing something they are saying could be off-putting to the crowd and causes them to lose the crowd. It could even be as simple as spending 30 minutes on one poorly executed PowerPoint slide that causes them to lose them. Whatever the reason, when they stop listening early, they can make a snap judgment about engaging on a new initiative. Even worse, the speaker will never really know because every time the speaker gets off stage and asks peers how they did, the common "nice" response they get is "great job." He thought in most cases a leader really will not know how the message is received until massive dollars have been spent, which was almost always too late.

The moral of the story is this. For there to be real communication and each side to feel valued, it has to go in both directions. Just listening to employees via some survey is not enough. If you think about it, a survey is really just asking a group of people to rate *your* ideas/answers from 1-10. It is not getting feedback from them in a way in which they get a chance to tell you how they felt or would have answered the question. Even open answer formats don't usually allow them to see each other's answers and collaborate.

It was clear to me leaders needed a new way to communicate. Most teams feel that the entire top-down communication and weight on their shoulders to please leadership is just too much. We figured that the solution for this was to get their opinion in an open answer format and to try to do it in a way that would allow them to be brutally honest but feel safe. The other critical piece was that we needed a way to for the conversation to build a common voice. Random opinions floating all over the place in an organization are so difficult to make sense of, left alone take action on. How could a leader know if the loudest opinion is the vocal minority or had 100s of people backing it? Voting helped solve this.

Weeks after working on the ROE problem with Jack, I was beginning to get clarity around what I wanted to do with the rest of my career. I wanted to help people Get Shit Done (GSD) by engaging with the masses via a tool that could drive adoption for evolution and change. I wanted to make a platform that could make the masses feel like they were accomplices in the master plan.

I will admit that in my enthusiasm, I did not truly realize how difficult the "Us vs. Them" problem would be to solve. Change is hard and reinvigorating apathetic or entitled audiences is even harder.

There are no easy answers, but I will share what we have learned so far about the pros and cons of crowdsourcing, the psychology of organizations, and how to operationalize engagement. We have worked with over 50 different large corporations at all different levels and while there is absolutely not a silver bullet, the progress we are making is astounding. By following the principle of "They Come First," where the employees are "they," and they have a voice and a way to be relevant, we can drive engagement. Engaged people produce leaps and bounds more than normal people and exponentially more than apathetic ones.

Bridges

The chasm exists and needs to be bridged with the right engineering. Leaders must understand the pain their teams suffer. They must seek the truth and make it safe to share it. We need to source and solve issues hampering the way forward in a way that extends accountability throughout the organization. We are not looking to be perfect. We are looking to methodically bridge the gap and drive adoption for scaling the business at every level in the organization.

Sourcing Pain

One year into developing our platform, in working with different companies, we concluded that the order in which we try to engage large groups of people matters. "They Come First" was this terrific altruistic notion, but it turned out that most of the time "they" were not always willing participants.

The epiphanies we had in our experience with Jack and "Rise of the Engineer" discussed in the last chapter caused me to start reaching out to other leaders. One of the first to want to try working with us on a use-case was Chris Laping, CIO at Red Robin Gourmet Restaurants. He was intrigued and had a great deal of experience with social collaboration tools like Yammer (purchased by Microsoft) and a few others. It was a great vetting point for me because I was not coming at the "Us vs. Them" problem from a technical standpoint. In fact for me, the psychology of it all was much more of a concern than how things would technically work. Chris, who is a well known speaker on change and change management, started schooling me in what he thought were the gaps with the current solutions out there.

Measuring Progress

One of the biggest issues with current approaches for bidirectional feedback is a lack of timeliness. Think about something as simple as a suggestion box. Write something anonymously on a card and drop it in the suggestion box. Have you ever wondered what happens to those ideas? Do they get made into paper airplanes and fly into some pile on someone's desk? No one really knows. All we know is that, more often than not, no action is taken.

© Hayes Drumwright 2017
H. Drumwright, *Management vs. Employees*, DOI 10.1007/978-1-4842-1675-0_7

Chris went on to talk about pulse and engagement surveys. Both are useful and have an application for management to learn a great deal about the organization; but from an employee's perspective, they feel like a large use of hours that go into a black hole somewhere. When is action ever taken on that feedback?

He felt there were products that allowed for good peer-to-peer collaboration out in the market; good horizontal apps that were especially useful for geographically separated teams. But when it came to vertical products, products that truly deliver access between leaders and the masses in a meaningful way, there was a huge gap.

Chris wanted to experiment with a "skip level" use-case that he thought would provide management access to different tiers in the organization and make it time-bound in order to deliver tangible results. He laid it out like this.

His President was going to have an offsite with the regional directors from all over the company in three weeks time. He knew that there were issues the regional directors were having from a process, technology, and communication standpoint that might not be making their way all the way up to leadership.

Chris had a hunch that issues lower down in most any company have a hard time gaining momentum and really filtering up in a way management was willing to hear let alone act on. They had tried town halls in the past, but the same 2-3 people always spoke up and seemed to have a pretty negative take on things. It was super hard in those settings to tell if everyone at the town hall agreed with them or they were just a vocal minority.

Chris wanted to run a session for his president sourcing pain from *all* of the regional directors. He wanted to get them all to speak up, even the quiet ones. He thought if they ran the session before the offsite, it would give the President a dashboard of issues he could use as his agenda for the offsite meeting. Chris decided since the meeting was face-to-face and accountability was a tenet at Red Robin that he wanted the regional director's names to show in the session.

He launched the session a couple weeks before the event and within three days had an agenda of issues he could hand to the President. The voting that occurred in the app gave the President a very clean list of the top ten things that were holding back the regional director's from being productive. Chris had successfully sourced pain from the group and would use the offsite for the President and team to validate and solve for the problem live.

Chris felt that action comes in many forms. Having a direct line (access) to the president and then being able to have intelligent conversation around the issues is absolutely a form of action. He did not feel it was imperative for his President to have all the answers. In fact, sourcing the issues for discussion not only streamlined the offsite, but by including the regional directors in solution discussions, they were able distribute the accountability.

We learned so much from Chris in watching how he thought through the process. It had never really occurred to us how important that feeling of access is to people. Most all of us want to feel like we are in the "inner circle" but have no idea how to access it. Chris' thought was to give all of the regional directors a way to access their President and then set the President up beautifully to validate that not only did they have access, but he heard them and cared about the things they struggled with.

I had never considered using the Portal of Pain to make an agenda for an off-site as Chris did for his president's town hall meeting. I only thought it would be good to create and drive initiatives forward by getting buy-in and adoption. I was thinking about my end goal as a leader, not my employees. I was putting the company first, not the people who made the company scale.

We boiled down the key lessons to this:

- Access matters to people.
- Crowdsourcing big issues helps leaders filter out the vocal minority and focus on the key issues.
- As a leader, having all the answers was not as important as acknowledging the problems.

So needless to say, we were excited. Chris got coverage in the *Wall Street Journal* for what he did with the Portal of Pain and I started to believe we were on to something. It was right around this time that we decided to change the name of the company to POP and brand the product POPin for "POP internal". I also let the management team at Trace3 know I was going to step down as CEO and work on it full time by mid year 2014. The goal was to brand POP as a company that could drive initiatives forward by getting buy-in/engagement from employees via the platform.

The key properties of the platform were to make it safe for employees to tell the truth to management over a 2-3 day time period and to drive accountability for solving problems down throughout the organization. Anonymous crowdsourcing gave participants the security to tell the truth. Being able to provide open answers (versus a 1-5 rating scale like a survey) gave them a voice in how to solve the problems.

Needless to say, we were excited. We had our basic tenets in place and some initial success so we started testing the value props in the market. Brian Anderson, POP's CMO, came up with the slogan "Actionable Social" to help differentiate what we were doing. The analyst seemed to like the differentiation as Jive and Yammer were being seen more as Social Noise due the lack of actionable content in the tools. We should have known with all this momentum we were bound to run into trouble…

What We Learned

One of our first clients was a very large international aerospace company. They wanted to run a collaboration session. Their question was how could they collaborate better across the different countries. They wanted to run the session for weeks and, not knowing any better, we let them. This killed the urgency around logging in. To make things worse, the audience of employees, instead of answering the original question, gave us the pain they were dealing with on a daily basis. It was good info to have, but management did not love it since they were getting responses that were off topic.

We chalked that experience up to being a potential outlier and pressed forward. Next we worked with a massive financial firm in the IT department. The first session was about innovation ideas and it went okay. Some good ideas floated to the top. The second session was around creating initiatives for continuous improvement and almost all the answers that were voted to the top revolved around pain. Management was frustrated. In fact, in a session asking how to find new streams of revenue, the item that got voted to the top was "meetings are killing us". The people that commented that back-to-back meetings were killing productivity and morale because people did not have time to even get to their next meetings on time let alone get work done. The POP team was fascinated by this and during our action planning session with the client, we handed them all Lencioni's book entitled *Death by Meeting*, thinking they would appreciate it. They did not. They thought the tool was not super valuable since they did not get answers they were looking for.

Within weeks of that, we had a CXO of a large company ask 1,500 people via POPin what the department's mission statement should be. *The session was a disaster.* They were asking 1,500 people to give them a one-line mission statement. To this day I am still not sure why I allowed that session to launch. There is little chance a question like that would work for completely open crowd-sourcing from that many people. Later, we figured out how to attack this type of a session with great results. You launch a session that has 5-7 finalists for the mission statement and let everyone vote and use the open comments to suggest minor content edits.

But this was not later; this was the beginning and with everything open ended we had duplicate answers everywhere in the app and voting was a mess because of it. It was hard to make sense out of any of it. After that session, they stopped calling us back. We were really bummed, because we had 3-4 good sessions then one disaster and the disaster killed us.

After these setbacks, we did some analysis and discovered some undercurrents at play. The process for setting up these time-bound micro social networks kept being challenged and even derailed by attitudes (psychology) we did not anticipate. *It was clear that in larger corporate settings, most employees had never had a chance to speak up in a meaningful way. "They" were ignoring the questions being asked and "barf-ing" whatever they wanted to say back uphill. When they did this, it seemed to reinforce management's belief that incorporating them in strategy development was a waste of time. I was fascinated by this and decided we needed to dig in.*

Why wouldn't our audience of employees answer the questions being asked? Well, when you step back and think about it, how often do employees get a voice? How often do they get do speak up and talk about what matters to them in an uninterrupted way? And even if they do get that chance, how many will panic when considering the political implications of what they say? At POP, we created a way in which they could speak their mind, mitigated the political risk, as well as give their peers a chance to support them. It turns out the employees did just that. In their first sessions, they had a strong tendency to express the frustrations they had around roadblocks, processes, and other things that made their job functions unnecessarily complicated. They naturally were more interested in talking about their issues than answering a question around something they did not think could tangibly benefit them. We decided to test our theory. What if we let them do what they had shown us they really wanted to do? We decided to experiment with letting them share their pain as the first step in driving engagement.

It worked even better than we expected. Before I get into a few use-cases, just consider your own personal view on the subject. How likely are you to take advice from someone that you don't think cares about you? How likely are you to go out of your way to help someone who you think does not care about you? Most of us—not all but most—don't put much credence in the advice of strangers let alone people they think don't like them. Who do we listen to and want to help? Most would answer family or friends or loved ones. We have their backs and they have ours.

They have our back. And we get theirs.

From those two simple sentences we derived our direction. Management, leaders, peers…if you want the help on problems and goals from your people, you first need to show them you care. We began giving critical thought to the kind of questions we could ask. In the process, we realized how you frame the question can be very important. We got creative and started asking questions like this: "What would stop you from referring a talented friend from joining the company?" or "What are the processes, systems, or roadblocks holding you back from being more effective?" Well, the first one might look like a question about recruiting, but it gives the participants a chance to say what they don't like about the job or department. The second question looks like "continuous improvement" but it also doubles as a way to voice in a safe man-ner things that are overdue for improvement.

In both cases, we are letting employees speak their minds about what matters most to them. As we listen and address the items that rise to the top, leaders are building a bridge by showing they care about what matters to their people. This will serve them well when the leader needs to ask for help.

Get their back, and they are more likely to get yours. That said, you don't need to solve everything they struggle with. In fact, that would be a mistake.

Pain Sourcing and Saying "No"

I would like to make the case that one of the strongest things a leader can do is source the largest pain points from her organization so she can get up in front of them and tell the group she can't solve the problems.

Let me give you a couple of examples of this in action.

Example #1: Large Healthcare Organization

We had a company approach us to help them better understand the results of a pulse survey they had run. The pulse survey had reported extremely low leadership scores for a certain leader in the org and HR wanted to validate why those scores were low, because his leadership thought he was doing a decent job leading his team. To get to the bottom of it, they ran a three-day session with the department asking the following question: "What are the biggest leadership issues facing this department?" They were informed the session would be anonymous and that, in order to improve the environment, their candid feedback was appreciated and needed.

At the end of 72 hours the dashboard from the session came in an overwhelming pain point voted to the top of the scoreboard. Over 90% of the department agreed that the biggest leadership issue was that the department had been understaffed and overworked for more than 10 months. It was hard to ignore the data when so many people in the department had voted on the idea. Some of the comments under the idea were even more telling. There were comments like "I have personally told the leader that we are understaffed and he said there is nothing he can do about it. This is unacceptable as all of us are working extra hours to get the work done." Another stated, "Our complaints about staffing have fallen on deaf ears" .

When the leader and HR got together the next day to review the results, the leader asked if he could hold an all-hands meeting with the team and have HR attend. They briefly discussed the plan and set the time for the meetings. The next day the leader stood up in front of the group and started off with an apology. He said he had heard their complaints about the staffing over the past 5-6 months and in the beginning had even tried to explain to a few of them why he couldn't do anything about it. As the complaints kept coming in from a few of the more vocal people in the department, he started to discount their validity since he had already explained his hands were tied. He admitted he had no idea it was such a large pain point for the entire group until he saw the dashboard.

He then did something very important. Something that everyone should take note of.

He took a moment to explain the constraints put on him as a leader in the organization.

We have realized that employees *rarely* if ever take the time to consider the constraints on their leaders. But with his dashboard in hand, our leader knew he had an opportunity. He was going to address an issue that was plaguing the group and he knew they would listen to him since the majority of the group had expressed pain.

He told them the following. Over the past 14 months three people in the department were on official leave of absence. While there was debate in the group around how legitimate the LOAs were, he had to accept them as legitimate since they were a very large organization and HR had approved them. The LOA policy was a two-year policy. The company had put it in place with good intentions trying to think of their employees first. The problem they were now discovering was that it was clearly having the opposite effect on the people who had to cover for those on LOA. As their leader, he would like nothing more than to backfill those people but he was not allowed to. He and HR had gone over the data and HR was going to do more research to understand if this was an issue in other departments.

He then apologized again for not communicating this well known policy to the group because he made the assumption they all understood it. He then did something smart. He told the group that he thought they were a very smart effective team and would like to ask for their assistance in solving the problem. He let them know he could not hire three more people and he could not change the LOA policy. But what he could do is run a new session and ask for their brains to help him figure out how to improve their work/life balance knowing the constraints he was under.

He stood up in front of them and told them he could not solve the problem. But in doing so he was able to explain the constraints, humanize himself, and gather them closer by including them on the brainstorming solutions. Six months later, on the next pulse survey, his leadership scores had more than doubled.

Example #2: New Leader Assimilation

We were working with one of the largest real estate mortgage companies in the United States and having tremendous success. We were working with a woman who showed tremendous leadership skills and had run a POPin session sourcing pain around communication with her team who was spread across the United States. The session was a big hit, word got out in the organization about what she was doing, and not long after she was promoted to the executive staff reporting COO and CEO. She immediately approached us and came up with a terrific new use-case for the platform.

Her suggestion was to use the platform to get a sense of what she was inheriting in the new department. There were 400 people in the group and they had been under the same leader for quite some time. The group had some of the highest engagement scores in the organization according to the HR engagement surveys, but the production of the group was lackluster. She wanted to dig into this so she could walk into the new role with her eyes wide open. She made her own selfie video joking that she was running for office (this was in an election year so the joke made sense) and she wanted to understand what her constituents needed from her. The video was humorous and approachable. She let the group know she cared about what they thought and how they felt so she was going to run an anonymous session in order to source the good and bad of what was happening in the department.

Three days later, the results were in. It was the highest level of engagement we had ever seen from new users. Our leader called me and sounded a bit frayed. The session stats were amazing and the entire group engaged and seemed to love having a voice. The problem was the voice was pretty unhappy if not downright disgruntled. There were problems everywhere and the sentiment from the group was management never listened and appeared to not care about them. The topic that was voted to the top of the session (by a mile) described how important it was that they be allowed to work from home. Those that commented on that topic (via the tools comments section) went as far as to say they would quit if the right to work from home was taken away. The next 4-5 topics at the top of the scoreboard were more manageable issues but also going to be tough to do something about. The reason my leader who launched the session was really worried was because the company was laying down an edict in two weeks that no one in the organization would be allowed to work from home any more…

I got in my car and was in her office later that day. She was a tremendous leader, but even for the best of us, this was a thorny problem. She was inheriting a disgruntled group and in her first announcement as their new leader she needs to give them horrible news on the matter they care the most about. When I walked into her office she took me to a conference room with a big whiteboard. We both knew there are no silver bullets for solving these kinds of problems, but at least we were not operating in the dark. We had data on what their issues were. We knew they were an underperforming group. We knew there were potential turnover issues. In fact, the number three topic on the scoreboard from the session was that middle management in the department was fat and needed to be trimmed.

They wanted to work from home, they didn't like middle management, they were underperforming as a group, information about their jobs and how to do those jobs was siloed so losing key people would hurt, and it also surfaced that the old leader who left to go to a competitor was recruiting the best people.

The first thing I did after we got all this on the table was congratulate her on the promotion. With the tension in the room, this got a huge laugh.

Clearly there was a lot that needed to be addressed. When we started to talk about an approach, she added for my benefit that she thought there were 6-7 gems (people) in the group. Most of these gems were in middle management in the group. We decided that we need to have a way to separate the people who wanted to step forward and help fix the department from those who wanted to sit back and complain about it.

She came up with a great idea having a town hall with the entire group and talking about the issues that rose to the top as best she could. We decided that we would leave the "work at home" topic to discussed at the end of the town hall. For the first part she discussed a process where people could opt in almost like a fantasy football draft to the topics they thought they could help solve the best. It was not mandatory to opt in, but the option was there if you felt you could be part of the solution. She announced that once the groups were formed, they would be launching their own sessions to dig deep into what it would take to solve the problems. There were murmurs in the crowd and she could tell she was starting to reach them. She discussed this process a bit more and let them know that each team would be responsible for suggesting solutions in a specific timeframe and she would hold herself accountable to working with each group so they could show progress around each issue every quarter.

She then addressed the elephant in the room and let them know that she had talked with the COO and CEO about the work from home edict and there was nothing she could do to change it. It was coming down within a week and she was sorry they had not gathered the data earlier on what a big issue it seemed to be. She let them know other leaders in the organization were beginning to crowdsource from their teams to see if they had similar sentiments. She had hoped that over the next couple of quarters they would have enough data to make a few exceptions, but there was nothing more she could do about it at the time. Then she honestly apologized that she was not there earlier to bring this concern more to the forefront for them as their leader. To her shock, they seemed to accept that answer and not hold it against her. It did not change the fact that it was an issue for the department; but with the way she started that town hall and the way she was inclusive instead of dismissive they accepted that she had made an effort.

When the town hall was done, the teams drafted themselves pretty quickly and helped her see where the real leaders were in the organization. They began zeroing in on improvements they could make.

Fast forward 45 days and I met with her again. They had decided as a group they were trying to do to many things. They were providing 10-12 services to the business at an average level and they had decided they wanted to provide 3-4 services at the highest level. They had almost completed reorganization of the department streamlining the services and building redundancy in order to protect the business and allow the top performers a chance for better quality of life, in and out of the workplace. To expand on this a bit: as the drafted teams identified solutions the negative people starting talking even louder and were easier to identify. As she streamlined the services she did make cuts to the address the negativity, but at the same time, she gave material raises to those who became part of the solution. She reallocated salaries from the negative to the positive.

The sourcing of the pain in the department gave everyone a voice in a way the leader could make sense of. Drafting the teams to attack the top problems pushed accountability down throughout the org.

The part I was most excited about was the execs all felt she had done the impossible in a record amount of time. She found the problems, created a solution, held the company line on changes, and had momentum to now build on a streamlined time that provided super valuable services to the business.

In both examples, we have an apathetic "they". In one, they did not understand the constraints on their leader. In the other, there was frustration around being disconnected. In both, employees were given a chance to express their pain and issues in a safe way. They did so immediately and once they did and they felt heard, both organizations could then move to creating solutions.

Our key takeaway here is that the order in which we solve problems matters. If "they" come first—that is, if we help them before ourselves—then we will have an attentive audience when trying to get engagement around our issues.

Truth Seeking

I was recently reading a book by CS Lewis who is most famously known for the Narnia series that includes *The Lion, the Witch, and the Wardrobe*. Those are not the books I am speaking of. He also wrote books for adults.

He had a brilliant mind and this book he wrote discussed some things that really gave me pause. If people look for comfort, in almost no instance will they find it. What they will find instead in most cases is something temporary and that will eventually lead to despair. In fact, the road to comfort is so difficult that many of us search for it for decades only to come up empty and alone. Pretty deep stuff.

He then explored what would happen if we did not search for peace or comfort, but instead were to search for truth. In that search for truth, we are to focus on making progress toward the truth every day. What would that entail? It would for sure have hardship. It would have roadblocks. It would have setbacks and failure. He thought it could be a very long road but it was the search for truth and truth only that was the only chance we had at finding true comfort.

The more I thought about it, the more I agreed. If we are honest with ourselves, we know that getting to the truth of matters is hard and often incredibly uncomfortable.

© Hayes Drumwright 2017

H. Drumwright, *Management vs. Employees*, DOI 10.1007/978-1-4842-1675-0_8

Here is a simplified example. We have all been to seminars or shows that have people on stage speaking to a crowd. Recently I attended one such show and there was a speaker on stage going through a rather detailed slide deck on an analytical topic. I was sitting next to some bright people and they were paying attention in the beginning but clearly started to lose interest as the speaker went from bullet point to bullet point on each slide. They even started joking that if the talk didn't end soon they would have to put headphones on. I felt for the speaker because clearly he had put a lot of work into the presentation deck, but it was almost unbearable and no one in the audience was paying attention.

As the speaker left the stage, he walked over and sat near us. I realized quickly that he knew the people I was sitting next to. He leaned over and asked them what they thought of the speech. One said he thought it was really good. The other people all started to nod in agreement saying it was a great talk. With this information the speaker smiled, stood up, and walked to the back of the room to take off his microphone. I guess I must have been making a face because one of them caught me looking at him, gave me a weak smile, and shrugged his shoulders as if to say "what was I supposed to say?"

A small shiver went through my body because my mind *immediately* recalled the tons of times I had walked off stage and had people run up to tell me how great my speech was. Crap! I thought. Were those people telling me the truth or were they just shining me on like these guys?

When it comes down to it, it is easier to just say what will make people feel good or get you out of an uncomfortable situation. And as the receiver of the news, it is easier to believe you were good and not ask follow-up questions to validate the initial feedback. I would bet most all of us have done this at some point or another. This is just a simple example where you could argue no one got hurt; comfort was maintained at the expense of truth.

Let's look at something that could be more dangerous. What if you were going to start a new business? Let's say you come up with a great idea and want to start a company to take it to market. What is the first thing we normally do in that situation? Well, I have done it a couple of times now. I go first to friends and family and ask them what they thought. Sound familiar? What do they usually say?

"Hayes, that sounds like a pretty good idea." Then I take it to more people and very rarely do I hear much negative feedback. So what should one do with this feedback?

Are we great speakers? Is our idea for the new company a great idea? I do not think you have enough information to know.

In sourcing information, you need to decide whether you are trying to source the truth or whether you are just looking for "goodwill." When the stakes are high, goodwill can cost you dearly. What if your idea for your company was only okay and not great, but no one has the guts to tell you because they want to be nice? You take their feedback as true, start your business using most of your savings only to realize that even the people who told you they liked the idea won't sign up and purchase the product once you develop it. Six months into the new venture you have burned through your savings, lost more than a few friends that you feel betrayed you, and have to shut the company down. Shockingly, this story happens all the time. All these people you sourced your feedback from on the venture were trying to be "nice" and that kindness ended up being a dagger.

The Road to Comfort Often Ends In Despair

I decided to place this chapter after "Sourcing Pain" because the entire concept of "They Come First" makes an assumption that not only are you willing to source the truth, you proactively seek it out. It is a prerequisite that leaders are willing to seek the truth and act on it to move forward.

I once gave a speech on the topic of sourcing truth vs. goodwill (which everyone told me was great...) and I joked in the beginning that it was a get-rich-quick speech. That got a good laugh. It is clear that many of us crave a fast way to create wealth and I could see people sit up a little straighter. Unfortunately for them, I then talked about CS Lewis and compared the "comfort" he talked about to seeking "riches" in business. Seeking riches will lead to despair the same way seeking comfort will.

There has to be a different reason you are starting your business. There has to be a different reason you are running a department. There has to be a different reason to go to work and contribute.

If you truly want to impact a market or have longevity, it must be an entity that at its core is in constant battle to find the "truth". I say battle because it is. It is a larger battle than I ever could have conceived. The truth has enemies and they are always trying to lull you into taking the easy path.

I argue that the truth for a company is value. If you are an entrepreneur, or a VP, or a CxO, or manager, or admin—whatever your position in the company—your goal must be to get to the core of what your customer values. Clients come in many forms depending on your position but once you key in to who they are, you must define what value is for them. Sometimes your client can help you find this truth and sometimes they can't. It is your job to be relentless about finding it.

Truth-Seeking Rule #1

Sourcing the Truth Involves Separating the Truth from Goodwill

Your job as a leader is to build a venture that will search for real value. It is to search for the truth of what your client really needs.

So you are thinking…Duh. I am not an idiot. But I can promise you something. There will come a day when you will have your leadership team at an offsite and everyone will be patting themselves on the back and making decisions that might temporarily make your venture more money, but they have stopped searching for value and your company will be closer to ruin each day. I promise it. It will be your job to help them step back on the road to value and the truth.

To illustrate how you can do this, I would like you to try a little experiment. I want you to find five potential customers and I want you to talk to them about the idea, concept, product, or service that you would like to offer them. I want you to sit down with each client separately and say something like this, "I am contemplating providing this service doing "X" and need your help. I would very much like you to tell me why I shouldn't do it. This is a big favor to ask of you, but please do it. I need brutal honesty. I am hoping you listen to the concept and explain to me why it won't work." I want you to do that. After you explain the concept, shut up. NO SELLING. There can be explaining, but don't start selling them.

Let's say they love it. They actually think you have stumbled on a real winner. Don't smile. Don't get excited. You see some version of this has happened to all entrepreneurs and what do we do? We run home we hug our spouse and start checking our bank accounts for what it would take to start this business that someone is talking you into starting. Could it be any better? I am going to ask you to please not do that.

We are on a search for the truth. We are on a search for real value.

If you have an amazing meeting and they convince you to do your idea, then say thank you and that you are trying to separate goodwill from truth. Explain that you are potentially about to embark on a very difficult journey providing this service from scratch and that it will take a great deal of time and effort on your part. (If you are starting a business let them know you are risking your personal wealth and the time you can spend with your family.)

So while they seem to like the idea you need them to go one step further. Ask them right there to pay for the service in some way. Not an investment, just to pay for the service. Consider it a prepayment for serious value that will be delivered soon. If it is not a product you planned on charging for… think of another way to figure out how much *real* value they see in it. I have started many companies and this is a *critical* question. Ask them for the money (or to prove value) right on the spot. All of a sudden a completely different conversation happens. It is a real conversation. One that drives progress toward the truth.

You will get all kinds of answers to this question and once again you will have the tendency to want to start selling them on the idea. Try to restrain yourself. A common answer is that they would need to see a couple of iterations first. Or maybe they need to see a bunch of other people using the service before they could commit to anything. Maybe they are just simply out of cash right now.

What is this experiment for? Why am I trying to make it so hard on us to step into the new offerings? It is because we need to establish a couple things before we start. Do they believe in the concept and would they give you some of their valuable time and effort to help get you an order for it? If they will, that is saying something about the true value of the offering. If they won't, that is saying something too.

The other really important thing you will discover with the second question is what they think of you as an entrepreneur or leader. This is more valuable than almost anything else. So many of us are asking our family and people that love us about whether we should start something new. We are going to get soft answers and a lot of goodwill from that group. When you test a new concept, make sure you test on at least half people/clients that do not know you. For those of you using this process to start a company if you don't know how to find those people then stop right there—you shouldn't start a company.

Truth-Seeking Rule #2

You Must Set Aside Your Pride

Besides taking the easy road to comfort, another deterrent to reaching the truth in value is our pride. It could be personal ego or pride you have in a product you created and have grown attached to. We could talk about well-chronicled companies like Kodak, Blockbuster, Blackberry, Nokia, etc., that at one time were all amazing innovators dominating their markets. All of these companies had incredibly smart people working there. They all saw the threats to their spaces via the likes of digital photography, Netflix, Apple, Samsung, etc., yet they were unable to turn the corner and compete.

Pride in what you have built can be a powerful thing. I have joked on stage that sometimes cannibalizing a product your company has made is so hard. The product feels like it is your baby and nobody wants to eat their babies. Yet sometimes, if you are really seeking the truth in value, you may come to the realization you have to. I don't want to trivialize this. It is so hard to do. I believe that is why so many truly great companies fall. Their pride in past successes causes them to seek comfort instead of the truth in value. They go blind and they fall.

There are certain things you can do as a leader that can help you stay on the path of truth even as you become more and more successful. Take the time as a leader to explain why it is you are doing what you are doing. For an example, when I ran Trace3 we wanted to strive for greatness and innovate the markets we chose to impact. That was our reason for existence. We also came up with a rally cry a couple years ago that we wanted to be relevant in the post VAR era.

For years, Trace3 had gone down a path and grown very successfully. But every year I would get with clients and do little truth-seeking experiments. I would ask them in a group dinner or one on one setting what they thought I should be worried about. Were there adjacent markets I should be considering? Were there things competitors we doing much better than us? Have we grown complacent? At one of the dinners, a bold client told me if Trace3 were to continue down its current path with our offering, we would be out of business within three years. Mind you, this was a good client. I stopped the dinner, like a needle scratching a record, and asked by a show of hands how many other clients agreed. Half the hands went up. I was floored. Next dinner with a different group, after a couple glasses of wine, I asked and got the same results. They all really liked the company and our culture, but an offering that had once given Trace3 terrific growth as an organization had hit a ceiling and was potentially going to be commoditized very rapidly.

In our search, we realized that even though we had grown from $100M-300M in two years that we might be sprinting right off a cliff. The team went to an offsite and I told them that it was very clear that we had to come up with plans and initiatives that would have two main goals. We wanted to secure the family (family being people at the company that truly worked hard and deserved to be there) and create massive opportunity. We eventually narrowed phrasing down to "Secure and Create". The reason for all initiatives could be explained in those terms.

After much thought and debate, I made the call to build two new practices and invest all the profits from the year into the bet. We would continue the old business, as it still had good play in the market, but we founded a cloud and big data team and started to look at how to add very aggressive advanced technology consulting on the best companies coming out of Silicon Valley.

Not everyone agreed with my plan. Almost half of leadership thought the clients might be wrong. They argued that Trace3 was just starting to make good money and we should bank it rather than invest it in new "Secure and Create" offerings. To be honest, there were even big parts of me that wanted to stick with the status quo. I had busted my butt to get Trace3 to $300M and would have loved to relax. Instead, I listened to the multitude of clients giving me the honest truth and made the executive decision to lose money for one year and invest in securing our future and creating massive opportunity.

Within a few months, there was a mutiny and I was asked to step down as CEO of the company I owned 100% of. I was told that I was always trying to change the company and people we tired of it. They were smart people. They were good people. They were by all standards incredibly successful people. They wanted to focus on the money on the table in front of them.

I'll stop the story right there because the point of the story is not to have you think anyone is good or bad for what happened internally at Trace3. The point is we had created massive success over the years and that success blinded some very smart people from listening to where the future value would lie. They were proud of what they built. It was working well. Blockbuster probably had similar fights. Blackberry too. Maybe even Barnes & Noble had huge knock down, drag out fights about what Amazon was doing back in the day.

Don't let your pride in your past successes blind you to how to protect everyone's future. Seek the truth in value and set your pride aside. You must always have a gauge on your current value and what your future value might be.

One of the simplest exercises you can do when you find yourself leading a team that has broken out into a civil war on which direction to go is this:

> Get a group of 10-20 clients together with your team members. Mix the groups up and then divide all the people into two groups. So in each group there are employees and clients (this can even work with just employees). Tell both groups they have two hours to leave the room and come back with a plan for how they would try to put your company out of business. What would the go-to-market offering look like? What changes would they make? Nothing is sacred. Put us out of business.

I have found the exercise helps them lay their pride aside and regain their truth-seeking glasses. It is especially helpful because many of the clients will have lots of good knowledge as to what the competitors do well. If you find your team split down the middle like mine was, give it a try.

Change is hard. It can be made even harder when you find out that progress toward the truth is not always racing forward as fast as you can. Sometimes it is; but sometimes it might be taking *really* hard feedback and completely retrenching something that is no longer working. Sometimes progress is doing a 180 and walking back to the start. Your guiding star on this is value and the truth. *Remember, if you are walking farther away from value toward money or something else that equals short-term gain, it will be a short walk.* I do not mean to trivialize this. In the moment you have to make this call, you can never know for sure you are making the right move and many times, you will be wrong. It is hard and there will be many hoping you might fail.

Truth-Seeking Rule #3

Failure Is Not an Option—It Is Necessary

Failures is part of the progress toward truth. Embrace the learning that can happen by failing and pivot toward real value. With many of the decisions you have to make, you will not have all the information necessary to be sure you are correct. In those situations you have a choice: act or be acted upon. My friend Tyler Beecher has a great story illustrating this concept.

ACT OR BE ACTED UPON –TYLER BEECHER

I'm pretty sure I was a great athlete in grade school. Yep, grade school! I was a playground legend, a big deal on my football team, and as a fifth grader I won the coveted Jr. Pentathlon (five track and field events). It had previously never been won by a fifth grader and I soon found my toothy grin in the local paper with enough individual and overall gold medals hanging around my neck to rival Mark Spitz. The sixth graders obviously weren't pleased, but I sure was. I went on to repeat the feat the next year and began to visualize myself on a box of Wheaties.

Then came seventh grade. I found myself entering a very large junior high school where to my amazement, no one heard of me and the few who had didn't seem to care. I, along with 70 or so classmates from my grade school, had been swallowed up in what seemed like a pool of thousands of kids. We were nobodies, and to be honest, it wasn't long before I didn't mind the anonymity. I had older brothers who passed through these prison years before and fed me tales of seventh graders getting pantsed, beaten, or even worse. To add insult to anonymity, I was now forced to use public showers after gym with a bunch of guys whose bodies looked like gorillas. Yep, my skinny, little goals had shifted from Wheaties spokesman to avoiding death by simian.

Just as I settled into my new goal of surviving, "it" happened. English class, third period. This horrifying girl who sat in front of me—I'll never forget her face—told me I was on the "hit list." It appeared I had caught the attention of the largest, meanest eighth grader in the school. He had a list of 10 kids who he believed deserved (and would receive) a beating at his hands. Now I won't venture to explain the logic behind who made his list, but I was somewhat honored by my ranking. Number three with a bullet. For just a moment I felt some pride return. I mean, according to this weird, mean girl, I was number three. She went on to show me her copy of the list, along with the names of the other nine victims targeted by this eighth grade thug. Apparently there were many copies of the list floating around school. My name was out there—I was back!

Unfortunately, my feelings of notoriety didn't last long. You see, Jerry (hairy gorilla executioner) gave a very public and serious beating to kid number one that afternoon. I was even taken to the scene of the crime to witness all the fresh blood drops. One of the minions even cited (again) how Jerry was going to beat each kid on the list after school each day. And in case I forgot, he stressed my number three ranking. My pride be damned.

To my dismay, Jerry made good on his word. The following day I witnessed a large kid (victim #2) sprinting away from school, bloodied and wailing. Day two and victim two scratched off the list. Tomorrow would be my demise.

Now I'd like to think if my kid were in this situation, he would come home and report this issue so someone/I could intervene. But things were different back then, and I fully believed if I told my parents, I would be viewed as "weak" by my brothers. I also believed telling my older brothers would result in them intervening the old fashioned way. I didn't like the way that story ended either. There was only one thing to do, so I spent the better part of that evening rehearsing my "final words" in the bathroom mirror, between praying my death would be both swift and honorable.

Following a fitful night, I got ready to head out the door for school and gave my mom an extra tight hug; same for my dog Poppy. I knew we would never see each other again. I was dressed in my favorite clothes, making sure I wore a shirt that would highlight any bleeding (my red badge of courage)—did I mention I was a little dramatic? As I was dropped off at school, what seemed like a hundred kids awaited my arrival. I distinctly remember one saying, "today is the day". Another giggled as he murmured "any last words?" It was on. Jerry clearly hadn't forgotten, nor had the rest of the school. I was a dead man walking.

My first few classes were tough, my mind anywhere but there. Then it hit me—English class, just before first lunch, me all cottonmouth and glassy eyes, staring into the mean girl's black mess of hair. Jerry and his crew of hyenas had first lunch. I had second lunch. But why let him pick the time and place of the fight? As the bell rang, instead of walking to my next class, I dropped my books at my locker and headed straight to the lunchroom. I opened the doors to face a chaos rivaling a trading door. I knew Jerry sat with his crew at the back of the cafeteria, so I jumped up on a bench and spotted their location. Then, I dropped back down into the crowd before they could see me. I felt my hands sweat, knees weaken, and I honestly couldn't remember one cool phrase I rehearsed in the mirror the night before. But I was committed and somehow, on legs losing strength with each step, made my way through the pandemonium to Jerry's table.

As I got close, they noticed me. No turning back. The gorilla's eyes fixed on me. His hyenas start cackling and smirking.

Now, I wish this story ended with me rolling up on this goon with a sock full of nickels and cleaning house. It didn't. What came out my mouth was nervous and overly respectful in tone, but somehow I muttered, "Soooo...I heard you're gonna beat me up after school today. If you have a problem with me, I say we get it on right here and now." Jerry locked eyes with me. And for a few seconds... nothing. Just him and me. Then, he muttered back, "We're good...I don't have a problem with you."

I believe I went on to compliment his Van Halen t-shirt and then turned and walked away. What I didn't realize in the moment was how quiet the cafeteria had become. All eyes were on me, and I did my best to exit with a bit of style (insides screaming—legs don't fail me now—don't trip!). My nightmare was over without a punch. Not a strong word exchanged.

So what's the moral of the story here? Was it about taking the fight to someone rather than waiting for it to be brought to you? Was it about calling the time and place of your shot? Was it about choosing to do something immediately that was going to happen eventually? To me it was simple. I was facing a clear and present danger and something visceral in my little seventh grade gut whispered it was better to take action than to wait and be acted upon. I have always believed the worst punch any of us will ever take is the one that is threatened but not yet thrown. For those of you who came from the tech manufacturing space where quarterly inspections/reviews are a regular part of the diet, you know those who wait to be acted upon (rather than acting) represent some of the worst scenes of professional carnage in many of our career memories.

This is such a great story and when you look at the macro message, you can see how you don't always know what is going to happen in life. You can only control so much of what is going on. The key is that acting is a stronger move toward the truth than doing nothing and hoping for the best. In Tyler's story, there was a clear and present danger in the form of a bully. In my Trace3 example, the clients "created" a bully that only half of my staff believed was real. In your businesses, I am sure there are real and phantom bullies all over the place. How do you decide which ones to act on and which ones can wait? There is no silver bullet answer.

Seeking the truth in value is a constant journey and one that involves trial and error. Sometimes progress toward the value means going against what is easy. You might even need to do a 180-degree turn. It is hard. It can be lonely. And sometimes the ones you love the most might even turn on you. Don't take it personally. Explain why you are doing it and that you know failures are part of the process. They key is to try to minimize the failures by setting aside pride and being honest with yourself and your teams about what isn't working. Use the lessons from your failures and pivot toward value.

There is no doubt that those leaders who choose to act will feel the pain of failure. But those who choose to be acted upon will feel the sting of eventual defeat.

I recently read this quote from John Burroughs:

> *"A man can fail many times, but he is not a failure until he begins to blame someone else."*

What a great quote. I lost my first company and I wanted to blame everyone but myself for that. Clients, the economy, lack of funding…But it wasn't their fault. It was my fault; 100% my fault. I let my previous success blind me to the fact that the market was changing. I stopped asking clients what they needed and started developing product in a vacuum. I stopped seeking the truth and instead went looking for riches. A goal of riches involves making compromises that will take you further and further away from real value. When the company finally did suffer true defeat because of my actions and I finally admitted to myself it was my fault, real learning and growth occurred and new companies were born with truth seeking at their core.

One of the hardest tenants of truth seeking to accept is that failure is necessary. That said, we don't have to love it. And I do believe we can take steps to minimize it.

Minimum Viable Stuff

My mom is an amazing baker. I think she might hold the land speed record for number of pies and cookies baked in an eight-hour period. She buys all the ingredients in mass quantity, sets up the grandchildren in an assembly line, and literally starts pumping out amazing desserts—chocolate, apple, and pecan pies along with hundreds of chocolate chip cookies. She is at the point that she no longer needs a recipe to bake; she can just do it by feel. She has been doing it for so long that each product she puts out is always baked to perfection.

Well, this is all true except for the one time that she didn't have any baking powder for the cookies. That time was funny and a little sad. The cookies didn't rise much. They looked like flat little chocolate chip pancakes. My mother was of course horrified when she saw the end product and wanted to throw them away. I mean this is a woman that holds her baking to a very high standard. The kids of course felt the need to taste the cookies and loved them regardless of their sad, flat shape.

The baker striving for perfection always sees the flaws in the end product. This often causes them to throw that delicious end product out and start over.

This little baking story is a poor man's illustration of two things. First, striving for perfection is admirable, but perfection is hard to reach. Second, your customers rarely need perfection. In fact, those kids would have been happy just eating the unbaked dough or the chocolate chips for that matter.

© Hayes Drumwright 2017
H. Drumwright, *Management vs. Employees*, DOI 10.1007/978-1-4842-1675-0_9

The term "minimum viable product" was coined by the great Eric Reis when he wrote the book, *Lean Startup*. I highly encourage anyone who has not read it to at least read the first half. It flies in the face of striving for perfection through long development cycles around new products. It pushes us toward letting the kids nibble on the chocolate chips while we are stirring the dough and then letting them nibble on some dough we set aside while the cookies bake. It says, deliver something woefully short of a full feature set and test how it is received…*a minimum viable product.*

I was so impressed after reading the book and listening to Eric speak a couple times I decided to try it on people. As we rolled out Secure and Create-type initiatives and services, we would try and roll out minimum viable versions at first. Many of them really struggled to get off the ground. I realized the big issues were goodwill and fear of telling the truth.

When leadership asks the opinion of their employees about something like a new initiative or service or even simple problems that need to be solved, there can be clear and present danger (read "a bully") for the employee. If that employee has negative feedback and it rubs management the wrong way, it could be career limiting. It is different than doing a focus group with clients where there is no risk for them. The employees have some serious potential downside.

I knew from reading *The Advantage* by Patrick Lencioni that there needed to be trust and conflict in order to get to the truth in value. We engaged with him on the issue and were able to get tremendous cohesion with teams of 8-10 people all across the company.

Lean Startup is terrific and *The Advantage* is masterful. What I learned from CS Lewis about truth seeking kept eating at me as the Secure and Create initiatives struggled. If we were going to seek truthful feedback and direction, we had to make it safe for employees to be honest with leaders. I needed one more piece to make it safe for employees. POPin had to be the truth-seeking platform that could make it possible for trust, healthy conflict, and a minimum viable iteration cycle to occur. So the basis for success with minimum viable stuff (MVS) is illustrated in Figure 9-1.

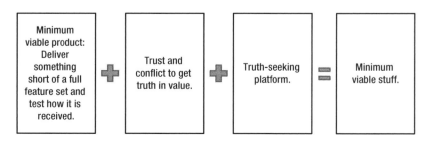

Figure 9-1. The basis of minimum viable stuff

In short, we are trying to figure out the shortest route to the "what" and drive accountability to those who need to do it. That could be a new service, an initiative, or any change necessary to help move the business forward.

Four Steps to Minimum Viable Stuff

In order to deliver on the promise of minimum viable stuff (MVS), you will need to approach the challenge in four stages: Discovery, Distribute Accountability, Pilot, and Iterate.

Let's take a look at each of these steps in detail.

Step 1: Discovery

I would love to make this complicated, but it isn't. Once management decides "why" they need to do something (be that a change, new service, offering, initiative, whatever), they need to do some recon about what would hold people back from engaging. The goal of the recon is to save time and money while giving management a better chance at success. As discussed in the previous chapters, the old way of doing this was to talk to people one on one. If you have no other option, this is not a horrible plan. You will just have to try to set it up so employees feel comfortable telling you the truth. If you can manage a way to do that, then you have to figure out a way to make sense of it quickly.

I was obviously so frustrated with how to do this that I stepped out of Trace3 to create POPin as the platform to make this easy. Engagement surveys had a place, but I had a heck of a time making sense out of them. Being able to ask the appropriate audience "what" stopped us from implementing a change, and getting answers ranked by the crowd in a couple days sounded like an awesome dream. Make it anonymous and let them vote on each other's answers. Only give them a couple days to argue about it and get you the answers. If as a leader you have a good idea "what" might stop the key players from engaging, you have a much better chance for success. Now that we have quickly crowd-sourced the "what" (the obstacles or the pain), let's move to Step 2.

Step 2: Distribute Accountability

In the Discovery step, we sourced what might stop us from accomplishing our goals. In this step, we will ask the appropriate audiences how to overcome what might stop us. *It is important that we accept in Step 2 that our solutions will not be perfect!* The goal is not perfection. The goal is to address the issues as best we can while driving accountability for solving into the organization. **Too often, upper management takes all the responsibility for solving problems and rolling out changes. This is doing the masses a disservice**.

Think of parents and their kids. Do you know parents who solve all their kids' problems? When parents do that, they do their kids a disservice. What have the kids learned? What will the kids be likely to do the next time that problem arises? Look at the other side of that. Do you know a bunch of kids who think their parents understand their problems? Any teenager reading this book is probably laughing. Oddly, that is the same laugh you get from people at the lower levels of a 1,000-person company. Management is just too far away to understand their day-to-day issues.

I believe management can help focus the company as to why things need to be done or accomplished. Achieving goals on an ongoing basis will take accountability and problem solving at every level. We need to train the organization to do that. In this step of MVS, we give the issues discovered in Step 1 to different teams and ask them to crowdsolve for them. They will do this over a couple days.

Could management do this? Maybe. Should they? Maybe there are special cases where they should; but as a general rule, asking different groups for solutions extends accountability throughout the organization. Over time, the hope is this ownership turns into engagement and creativity throughout the company.

Step 3: Pilot

Once we have crowdsourced "what" could hold us back and crowdsolved "how" to attack the issues in a quick time-bound manner, we want to take the product/service/initiative/new process/solution to market. We are not taking it to market because we think it is completely baked and perfect. We are taking it to market to test it.

I titled this step "Pilot" because I want to drive home that nothing is ever baked. *Ever.* Whether that pilot is rolled out to 10 or 10,000 people, it can always be improved. The most successful plans after three months of being in the market can always be improved. Pilots will give you more data with which you can improve, provided you can make sense of that data. So whether you consider Step 3 of MVS a company-wide launch or rollout to a smaller target audience, always think of it as something that will need iteration and improvement.

Step 4: Iterate

You want to have plans to repeat Steps 1-3 in a specific timeframe. One recommendation to increase the effectiveness of driving accountability into the organization is to delegate iteration to various teams. Regardless, iteration is like insurance in the money invested in the growth of your business. It is a strong cultural message that status quo is not good enough and continuous improvement is mandatory.

It is the "Iterate" step that hopefully makes you more comfortable rolling out initiative/services/changes that are not perfectly baked. With the right ideas, as outlined in the *Lean Startup* and *The Advantage* books, and a platform like POPin, we should be able to accomplish change and constant improvement in a way all levels of the company can engage.

Let's look at a real example.

MVS in Action

We were working with a very talented leader who was the VP in sales management at a Fortune-100 cable company. Our leader came up with a concept for a sales initiative called 5-5-5. The sales organization was nationwide and had seven regions. The "5s" represented the booking, processing, and closing of five orders per day in each region. The "why" behind the initiative was pretty clear: if they were to accomplish 5-5-5, they would service their clients better. All key revenue metrics would be hit and the growth would allow them to add headcount and obtain more capital budget. There was zero disagreement as to what success would look like but there was a great deal to be figured out as to how they could reach the goals in a methodical, repeatable fashion that could be embraced and understood by the over 600 sales people in the trenches.

We decided early on that while perfection would be a wonderful way to start, it was probably unrealistic. In fact, with macro-economic factors playing into a 12-month initiative, it would make sense to be checking in on a quarterly basis to see if we needed to make tweaks. With this in mind, we decided we would do the best we could to identify the key ingredients for success and then validate them as quickly as we could. We wanted to do all of this in a 4-6 week period.

Step 1: Discovery

Rather than distract the entire division and try to overbake the initiative, we went to the first three layers of management (80 leaders) and crowdsourced an answer to the following question:

"What are the systems, processes, tools, and methodologies in place today that will hold us back from accomplishing our 5-5-5 goals in the next fiscal year?"

This was a terrific question because this team of leaders had lived this problem and had a deep understanding of the shortcomings they dealt with on a daily basis.

After three days he had sourced from all 80 leaders across the country and over 100 answers were entered into POPin by the group. As a result, seven of the top ten jumped out as key issues.

Our leader had seven regional directors (RDs) so he assigned one of the seven problems to each of them. He gave them these instructions. He said he wanted each RD to brainstorm solutions to their assigned problem with a small group of their choosing. He gave each of them 2-3 days to make this happen. They were not to use technology for this.

As each of the RDs met with the leader to discuss the outcome of their brainstorming sessions, the leader posed a few questions. First, whom did they pick to brainstorm with? Second, how much conflict was there in the brainstorming session? Third, how confident were they that their solutions would work?

When he told me this I had to smile. He said each of the leaders were on their heels a bit with these questions. As it turned out, most all of them brainstormed with people they thought were smart, but whom they also got along with. There was not a ton of argument. That said, most all were confident they had come up with the correct solutions for each problem.

Stage 2: Distribute Accountability

He had each of his seven regional directors make a selfie video explaining the problem they had been assigned. Then he had each of them launch a crowdsolving session to have all 80 managers give their thoughts about how to solve for the problem. This is roughly the same assignment he had given each of the regional directors to brainstorm. He told each of the RDs to seed their brainstorming answers into the crowdsolving session to be voted on. Since the platform was anonymous, none of the 80 leaders would know who entered what and therefore certain answers would not get special treatment or favoritism in the voting. It was his little experiment to see if the traditional way they had been vetting ideas was effective or not.

In all seven cases, not once did more than two of the brainstorming solutions even make it into the top 10 solutions. Each of the RDs had a completely new appreciation for sourcing and solving from a larger audience who felt safe in answering honestly.

Stage 3: Pilot

With the sourcing and solving complete, they felt they had an initial plan of action to launch 5-5-5. They were aware they had not reached out to all 600 sales reps, but they felt the most strategic minds had been involved in the creation of the initiative. They felt that involving the reps would have been too distracting.

Stage 4: Iterate

After three months the leader made a video for the sourcing session explaining why 5-5-5 was so important and asked the reps to give him honest feedback. He said he knew when they rolled out 5-5-5 three months previous that it was not perfect. He told them that he knew they (the people in the field) were the ones that 5-5-5's success depended on and he wanted to hear from them about how to iterate it for the better.

The reps joined in and gave feedback. The management tier were once again assigned the key problems and ran solving sessions. They then did their iterations as needed. This has continued each quarter of the year. The steps of MVS get you to the truth of "stuff" very quickly. With Distributing Accountability as the second step, MVS also helps you with the most difficult part of finding the answers the teams will embrace.

Our feedback from the leader in this case study was that *he felt all he had to do was explain "why" the initiative was important and his management layer came up with how to do it.*

"It was the least amount of time I had ever spent creating an initiative and the greatest amount of buy-in I have ever had rolling one out."

With MVS we had given management the opportunity to bake something of value and roll it out in a timely manner. Not having everything perfect, we gave the trenches a chance to get in on the process and buy-in to accomplishing the goals.

I know that MVS can seem like a big process. Most of my favorite examples of it being used are big too. They don't always need to be. It can be used simply to ask people what they thought of a speech.

A $7,000,000 Insurance Policy

I once had a client tell me they spent $7,000,000 on an offsite meeting for their entire company. I almost spit out my Dr. Pepper (so much better than coffee). All-hands offsite meetings are meant to do many things. In this case, the $7M was spent on the top five layers of the organization. This was a company with many, many layers. The goal was to lay out the mission, vision, and initiatives that would make the company thrive in the next 12 months. They wanted to get leaders all over the world pumped up about the company as well as give them a real understanding of where they were headed.

When the meeting was over and the $7M was in the wind, the leaders were supposed to go back to their locations all over the world and spread the good word about where the company was going and how their location/department was relevant in that plan.

After cleaning up the Dr. Pepper I had spit out, I asked my client this. "How did he know they went back and delivered the message correctly?" Even better, "How did anyone know whether spending the $7M and having everyone attend worked? How did they know they received and internalized the messaging in a way they could then deliver correctly to their teams?" I mean, it is not exactly like making a $7M prayer; but if you spend that kind of money on an offsite, don't you want some assurances the message got through and would carry forward correctly?

What if we asked them? Consider "asking them" like an insurance policy for the $7M spent. We could ask something like, "Hey, thank you all for giving us four days of your life. We just presented a ton of information to you. Please join this crowdsourcing session and let us know if a topic or message didn't make sense to you and you need more clarification before bringing it to your teams."

You could also get feedback on speakers and specific topics, find out whether they thought you missed covering something vital, etc.

The key is, if you are going to spend millions, be sure the audience understands the messages and can carry them forward correctly. If you don't, how much time did you waste at that offsite? And even worse, how much time will be spent cleaning up the bad messaging that occurs after the fact?

You don't have to be the person giving the speech for this example to be valuable. You could be part of a team and ask your peers in a group format about something you did not think was clear. You could even start conversations with the speakers about parts that you found confusing. This story illustrates the discovery piece. Give some thought to what you can do with the discovery data to push accountability for cascading messaging from an offsite through the organization as the second step. Hopefully things immediately jump to mind.

If the purpose of MVS is to source the "what" and distribute accountability for the "how" then what we are really talking about is driving engagement. By applying the methodology, we are helping the top connect to the bottom in the big plays; but we can also help the middle connect to the middle and serve each other better. Here are some other ways to leverage MVS.

Project Management

Probably one of the simplest ways to apply MVS is to iterate current projects. You can initiate pre-mortems, checkpoints, and post-mortems. Normally once a project is up and running we just do spot checks to discover problems or roadblocks, but applying crowdsourcing and solving will help get much more valid data in a time-efficient manner. As pointed out in the 5-5-5 example, spot-checking is not incredibly effective or safe for the people answering the question.

New Leaders

We have had new leaders join companies and use it for "new leader assimilation" at the CxO level. This can work at absolutely any level in an organization. When leaders take over a new department, they use MVS to better understand what they are inheriting and how to help their employees.

Many More

Without boring you, there are all kinds of ways to apply MVS to move forward. You can use it build agendas for meetings, gather projects for capital budgeting, dig into pulse survey results, and even solve retention and leadership issues.

I had originally written all these different MVS use-cases down, but as I reread them I realized it really starts to become intuitive and doesn't need so much explanation. Just think of a process, system, or problem you want more engagement on and apply the methodology to it. It really is that simple.

Accidental Adoption

There were some unintended consequences of working with many different companies applying the MVS methodology. As they quickly began to dissolve the "Us vs. Them" divide between leadership and the employees, they started to ask about customer and partner use-cases. I also saw potential to bridge engagement gaps with customers/partners since they are audiences any company must serve to successfully scale. Therefore, we gave it some thought and decided to look at all our assets and see what we could test for those that were asking. The Nucleus is where we started.

The Nucleus

I have one more company I have yet to mention. It is a group I have begun to put together called "The Nucleus". When combined, Trace3, InstantScale, POPin, and the Nucleus come together to create something special. I wish I could say that I had a master plan to create the picture that is now forming when you combine these pieces, but if I am honest, being opportunistic and open to learning (and failing) is in the end the secret sauce that made it all happen.

© Hayes Drumwright 2017
H. Drumwright, *Management vs. Employees*, DOI 10.1007/978-1-4842-1675-0_10

I have worked with some pretty smart people in my career and two in particular helped devise a plan for the Nucleus. Their names are Susana Sipkovich and Russell Bacon. Susana worked at Trace3 (along with Chad Cardenas and Drew Cather) to devise and mature the original "VC Briefing" program that would take CIOs and their directs to Silicon Valley to speed date with entrepreneurs. Russ came from DirecTV as the Chief Inspiration Officer to join POPin. Here is the problem they decided to attack.

InstantScale used the VC briefings as a vetting point. If a lot of clients liked a certain startup and wanted to purchase their products, Trace3 would notice and report to InstantScale that they should consider investing. In order for Trace3 to have enough data, 10-20 weeks would have to elapse since each VC briefing involved flying entire client teams (CxO and their directs) to Silicon Valley. Russ and Susana decided this was too slow. Trace3 had over 2,000 clients. They developed great relationships with Silicon Valley VCs. We had an investment vehicle at our fingertips via InstantScale. And we also had this cool crowdsourcing platform at POPin.

Well, what if we were to take 100-200 CIO/CTO/CDO/CISOs from Fortune-500 companies and crowdsource from them feedback on product features, go to market strategy, and company feedback via POPin? Russ and Susana came up with a template to professionally film each Silicon Valley entrepreneur delivering the following content—the problem statement, solution, 2-3 use-cases, and the question for the Nucleus to answer. The video would play at launch in POPin and in *two days,* the startup and InstantScale teams would know how hundreds of companies felt about these startups. Two days to access a very powerful group of people.

Why would this work? Let's look at the benefits.

Entrepreneur—The key word here is access. Not on-stage access but actual dialogue via the platform that gives them *critical* feedback to make pivots in their A and B round stages. With this feedback they save incredible amounts of time on features, direction, and messaging. As any founder will tell you, the best funding is always from clients so even though they cannot reach out to the Nucleus members directly (they can't solicit the group), the Nucleus execs can opt in themselves to further the conversation. Big win for the startup.

Nucleus Members—The execs save time accessing innovation. They get to see a new company every three to four weeks and it takes only 5-10 minutes out of their schedule. They can do it on the couch with a glass of wine. Given how over-utilized they are, this is a huge win. They also get to see what all their peers think. Some may have experience with the startups' products and getting that input from peers they trust is hugely valuable. They get access, they get say about direction, they save time, and they get to be the heroes for finding game-changing technologies.

InstantScale—10-20 weeks for vetting is cut down to two days, all the while gathering even more conclusive data. Enough said.

Trace3—With this type of access they can decide what products are key to building expertise around even faster than before, which helps them stay ahead of the market and make the CxO clients feel like they can see the future and look like heroes.

POPin—At the request of the Nucleus members, we added a "clone" feature that worked almost like a re-tweet. We called this feature a RePOP for repopulating a session to a different audience. If an exec loved a new startup, she could RePOP the video/question and relaunch internally in her organization to vet how viable rolling it out internally would be without ever having to deal with sales reps. Now POPin has become the Trojan Horse for discovery and distributing accountability.

Memento Mori—Okay…I have no reason to list MM here, but I felt really bad keeping it out of the master plan. We do host Nucleus dinners and pour the wine. I know, that is weak, but I am counting it.

Accidental Adoption (Not the Baby Kind)

Creating the Nucleus had an amazing unintended consequence. Art Gilliland is the CEO of a company called Skyport Systems. When we made Art's video for his Nucleus session, we immediately liked him. He was previously at HP and had taken over Skyport before their B Round of funding. We launched Skyport's session with the Nucleus and 84% of the CxOs who logged in wanted to talk more with Art. We (at POPin) were shocked. We had never seen better than 24% of the members wanting to move forward. Then, to my amazement, Art personally did all the phone calls and meetings. No delegation. The meetings went well and as Trace3 started to work with Skyport on getting orders, InstantScale got our allocation to follow Google Ventures (the lead investor) and invest in Skyport's C round of funding.

I then received a call from Art. He had talked with some people at HP about what had happened with his Nucleus session. He had explained how, with a five-minute video that Russ and Susana had produced, he had gotten discovery type feedback from many clients in just three days' time (not to mention follow-up meetings).

Me, being dense, said thank you. Art told me the following, "Hayes, think about it. HP, Cisco, IBM, Dell…they all buy companies. They have so many different offerings. When they acquire a company, how do they drive adoption with the sales teams? Cisco alone has over 15,000 sales people! What if you could move adoption rates from 10% to 20% by having a video like the one you made for Skyport? How many hundreds of millions could that mean for companies that are trying to integrate acquisitions?"

Me, still dense asked, "How would that work?"

"A company could use the video as a means for delivering a consistent message throughout the entire organization and ask the various groups (sales, engineering, etc.) 'What would stop you from integrating this product into your sales process?'. After that discovery is done and they know the objections they could solve the big ones. But that is not what they are really excited about. If a rep really likes the acquired offering and had a way to deliver that message to a group of clients quickly and effectively in a way the clients could give him feedback on interest levels…"

I got it, "You mean like letting each HP rep create his own client Nucleus and clone the session to save time and find out who is interested (without having to personally be an expert on the acquired offering)…"

I could hear Art's smile on the other side of the phone.

He had figured out how to drive adoption and engagement both inside and *outside* of a company's walls to its sales teams, clients, and partners. I started calling people I knew at Arrow, Cisco, Venture Firms, and other companies. We found the Nucleus model applied to mangers of advisory boards, product mangers needing to test potential offerings, and M&A teams looking to drive adoption.

There is so much more I could add about the potential of this application of a Nucleus-type model, but I want to try to break down the incentive models each audience might need.

Audiences Outside of the Company

It takes different tactics to engage with different audiences successfully. I use a sales modeling story to illustrate a potential strategy for engaging different audiences.

As I was building out my financial models when I was raising money for POPin from VCs, the dreaded question comes, "How many months do you want to say it will take to ramp a rep?" I always want to say six months, but I know that it is more like 9-12. No matter the training or level of mentoring, it seems enterprise reps always take a year to hit stride.

It is a tough problem to solve. After 15 years of working on it, I might have just figured out a way for us crazy entrepreneurs to let our CFOs believe in us and put a 5 or 6 in the Excel cell for "months to ramp a rep".

Different Incentives for Different Groups

There are three steps to ramping reps quickly that I think will illustrate how to appeal to different corporate audiences:

- *Identify pain:* Crowdsource your issues and establish priorities
- *Find the carrot:* Determine the best motivational incentives
- *Use your stick:* Relentless attention to detail

Let's take a look at each of these steps in detail.

Step 1: Identify Pain

This is the piece you know.

In order for there to be speed and efficiency, there needs to be trust. When you hire a group of new sales people, one of the best things you can do after they have been in the field for 30 days is to crowdsource pain from them over a 48-hour period. Find out what their biggest roadblocks are to succeeding and moving faster. What do they not understand about the product or service? What objections are they struggling the most with? Are there internal processes they don't understand?

The crowdsource aspect of it is the technology piece. It builds a common voice versus a vocal minority. With this data, you can stand on solid ground knowing you are helping as you remove roadblocks. Obviously this works for every department, but I have found the sales sessions can give you a hard ROI so I like starting there.

The human aspect of this move is to prove you are a leader who cares about their success. Yes, it is self-serving because they ramp faster, but you are taking time to show them that their success matters to you. This is more powerful than you realize. It is banking trust so when you have a really challenging MBO or initiative, they will go above and beyond to help you achieve it.

Step 2: Find the Carrot

This step is about opt-in and speed. It is *client-focused* and exposes how untapped they are to help ramp your salespeople.

Go to your 20 best clients who use your product or service and offer them something. Offer them the ability to help shape the offering in a concrete way. Tell them you are starting a customer advisory board, but not like one they have been on before. This one is going to offer four simple things:

- *Access:* You will give them behind-the-curtains access to product development and go-to-market strategy.

- *Time savings:* You will be asking them to join a crowd-sourcing session once a month and watch a 3-5 minute video. The video will state a problem, your angle on the solution, and then ask an open-ended question as to what they think of the problem and solution. It will take a total of 30 minutes once a month.

- *Peer-based transparency:* In the session they will be able to see what all their peers think about the problem and solution. They will be able to discuss their problems knowing the crowd is like-minded since they see value in the products offered as users.

- *What is in it for me?:* This is the most important part. I know now after a year of running crowdsourcing sessions with employees and clients that getting them to participate is the real challenge. You *must* have an incentive for them to participate. You will know your industry best and what a good incentive looks like, but here are some simple examples: Annual discounts on purchases, meetings with your executives, annual offsite for CAB members only, access to industry thought leaders (you pay to have them speak for them), etc.

If you do this well, once the CAB is built and you have a successful crowd-sourcing product and go-to-market direction, your opportunity will arise to truly help sales.

First, these clients are now bought in to your strategy and product direction. This should greatly shorten sales cycles. Second, if the group is gelling, at the six-month point, you should be able to ask each of them to refer 2-3 other companies (peers) into the group. Their referrals are the best possible leads you can get to your younger reps who are trying to ramp up.

The last point on this—you can have CABs with different functions. Executive, Marketing, and Technical CABs are all possible depending on what your product or service does. Crowdsource from each, give them incentives, and build the network to help sales.

Step 3: Use Your Stick

We covered how to help employees directly and how to get clients to help drive sales. *The last important asset is your partners.* Many of us have partners who help drive our businesses forward. Our partners often have a better sense of our company's weaknesses than our clients or employees do. They can be a goldmine of information. Set up partner advisory boards and crowdsource from them as well. Most all the steps I described for the clients are also true for the partners. The one main difference is that in my experience they respond better to a stick rather than a carrot-type incentive.

Many companies give some sort of co-op or funds to partners that perform well for them. I am not saying to pull any of those incentives. I am advising that you make it a requirement of your incentive program that in order to get the funds/incentives they must log into crowdsourcing sessions and give you feedback on strategy, go-to-market direction, product, and pain. Pain is where I would start for the reasons I stated in the employee section. Always build trust first. Partners can help your new sales people access new and existing markets. Make it a required part of the partnership that they help…and they will.

Leaders Need Followers

You have a daily choice whether you will act or be acted upon. Building followers for your cause doesn't have to be difficult. There are simple things you can do as you set out to "become" something in or with your organization. This process involves appetizers before entrees, eating babies, doctors, preaching failure, MVS, and choosing a path. Don't worry—the babies thing is more about cannibalism than it is babies. Sorry, that probably didn't help alleviate the worry. Maybe just keep reading and it will make sense.

Being versus Becoming

The subject of expanding people's capacity intrigues me, especially if it involves people I care for the most. How can you help others do it? To help them, I tried do it for myself first. Four companies later, I now feel I can attempt to write down what I have learned.

People always claim not to have enough time and the smart ass in the bunch never fails to say, "We all have the same amount of time. It is what we do with it that counts." I find myself saying that to my kids every now and then, which I guess makes me the smart ass.

But many studies show the effects that lack of time has on our ability to be creative and productive. There is a terrific book called *Essentialism* by Greg McKeown. It talks about saying no to things we normally say yes to in order to create more time for ourselves to focus on the *thing* we need. Not things, but thing. It is worth the read. It helps people see that their actions are the problem. How "busy" we keep ourselves is an issue to our moving forward in work, happiness, and life. At work, I do think employers are as much to blame as employees, but the angle I appreciate in *Essentialism* is that we do have a great deal of control over ourselves and can make changes to get capacity back.

© Hayes Drumwright 2017
H. Drumwright, *Management vs. Employees*, DOI 10.1007/978-1-4842-1675-0_11

This leads me to my argument on "being" versus "becoming". I gave a speech about this in 2014 and while it wasn't specifically about finding more capacity in life to become something sharper and better than your previous self, it plays off some of the same tenets. The concept sparked in my head in my early 20s. I watched so many friends and co-workers sitting around being something. I also watched a special few push and start becoming something more than was expected of them. I decided more than anything, being versus becoming is a state of mind. It is striving for more, not for the sake of more, but to push yourself to try and realize your potential. To challenge what is possible. Partially for me, it is a way to feel truly alive. If this is too sappy for you, let me go back to how the spark first started in me.

I remember sitting in a doctor's office when I was 20 years old. The year was 1993 and I was attending Boston University. It was the first semester of my Senior year and I had just been voted Captain of the Men's Swimming Team. I felt young and pretty invincible. I had a problem, though. I had actually had the problem for almost three years, but in the last 2-3 weeks before I went to visit this particular urologist, things had gotten much worse.

At 17 I had a lot of stomach issues. I also noticed that I had a lump in a spot I should definitely not have a lump. The lump was tiny and in comparison to my digestive problems did not seem like a very big deal. I went and saw a General Practitioner. He told me that maybe I was spending an hour in the bathroom each morning because of my diet. I told him that no matter what I ate, I was having issues. Pepto Bismal and anything else I took was not making it any better. I also told him about the lump. He told me I was young and not to worry about it.

At 20 the stomach issues were sporadic and I had learned how to handle it a bit better. The lump, on the other hand, suddenly had a life of its own. It was on my left testicle and over a 10-day period the testicle hardened and grew in size. Clearly something was wrong and I went and saw a doctor on campus. He checked it, thought it was strange, and gave me antibiotics. I think it was amoxicillin. On the third day of my taking the drugs, the testicle got even harder and then started to pulse. The pulsing was the first time it had hurt. It freaked me out. I called my mom who was a registered nurse at the time. She yelled at me a little for being an idiot and not seeing a specialist. It was 8:00pm in Texas (where she lived) when I called her yet somehow she found me a top Urologist in Boston. The next morning I rode the T 45 minutes to his office. I was sitting on the table with that crinkly paper on it when he walked in. He checked me for about 45 seconds. I watched his face and it gave away nothing. He sent me downstairs to an ultrasound tech. I have to admit that was pretty weird. The tech puts the gel on you and then starts gliding one of those paddle things on the gel and it puts a picture on the screen.

At first I thought it was one of those paddles they charge for shocking people that had heart failure and almost freaked out. He assured me it wouldn't hurt, but he turned the screen so I couldn't see the picture. I watched his face closely too just to see if it would give away a hint of how bad my situation might be. He squinted a bit, tapped some keys on the keyboard, but didn't say much. I asked him how it looked and he said he was not allowed to comment nor qualified to diagnose anything. I tried once more to get him talking and he once again said I would have to talk to the doctor.

One of the reasons I was nervous is that my good friend Adam, who I swam with at BU, told me he had a friend in high school that had a problem like mine. He said his swelled up to grapefruit size overnight and the next day he found out he had cancer. That made me nervous. My mom thought it was a hernia. I really had no idea what that was, but it sounded better than cancer.

The ultrasound tech sent me back upstairs and I was once again crinkling on the table/bed thing in the doctor's office. I just sat there by myself for about 15 minutes. I remember being more interested in what was going on rather than being scared. I think at 20, you just assume not much bad can happen to you.

When the door opened, two doctors walked in. My heart sank to the floor. My doctor introduced me to the other doctor and we shook hands. Time moved very slowly in that moment. My doctor looked me right in the eyes and said this, "Hayes, I want you to understand something. Please hear me when I say this. I have never lost a patient to this. Never. Hayes, I am so sorry but you have cancer. It is testicular cancer and it has a 97% cure rate. And once again I have never lost a patient to this."

I responded in shock, "Umm…when do you think I will be back in the pool?"

He replied, "Hayes, you will not be going back in the pool for a while. You have cancer and we need to act quickly. This other doctor will be doing surgery on you in two days to remove the tumor. Most likely after that we will start very aggressive chemotherapy. If it turns out the cancer has spread we will need to do another surgery and remove all the lymph nodes in your abdomen and chest. This is serious and I need you to understand we will do everything to beat it. But swimming, college, and life in general must go on hold for now."

I remember a single tear running down my right cheek. After that it gets a little blurry. The next thing I remember is the doctor calling my mom. It was a green phone he had in his office and it was one of the old school ones that had a cord on it and the big handset like you would see on the rotary dial phones. He explained that I had cancer, not knowing that she had lost her second husband to cancer just years before. I had not really cried yet, but I heard her wail. It was a drop-to-your-knees type of anguish I had never heard before. I could hear it and I was not even holding the phone. The doctor looked at me with a sad face and I completely lost it. I started bawling and he reached over to the Kleenex on his deck and handed me the box.

Think about this doctor and what an amazing man he was. He truly lived "They Come First." The first thing he said to me and to my mom is that he was going to take care of me; that I was going to be under his watchful eye and he had never in his entire career lost a patient to this cancer. That is a risky statement for him to make with malpractice and the like. But he made it. He gave us the truth of it sprinkled with a serious dose of hope. I am not sure I could have been luckier than to have him. I was completely alone, almost an hour from my close friends, and there was no such thing as a cell phone back then.

He kept me in his personal office until I stopped crying, talked to my mom as long as she needed, and then called my dad and did the same. He was a very special man in my life. His correct diagnosis saved my life. And he basically told me he was going to save my life within minutes of meeting me.

Needless to say, in that exact moment, sitting on that crinkly table, everything changed. My life would never look the same. From that moment on, I knew that everything could be taken from you in a single sentence. *If* you lost your health, you could lose everything. Failure did not matter. Being embarrassed did not matter. Trying and coming up short did not matter. Only losing your health mattered in the grand scheme of things. Even difficult relationship decisions seemed easier to make. If you were healthy, then you had time. And with time it seemed anything could be achieved or recovered. It is from that experience I decided I would do everything I could to *become* something. I did not want to take a negative view of having cancer at such a young age. I saw it as a wake-up call from just "being" part of what everyone expected.

When I left college and returned home, I immediately started a little venture with my brother called Holiday Highlights. It was simply putting holiday lights on people's houses for money. In its fourth year, my brother had over $70K in revenue in the months of November and December. I still remember our first customer. We had made fliers and left them on cars in a parking lot. Someone called and we went to their house with a Polaroid camera. (For millennials, that is a camera that produces a tangible picture you can hold within 20 seconds of taking it.) We took a picture of the front of her house. I then got a red felt tip pen and drew for her where we would put the lights. She said it looked great and asked how much. My brother and I looked at each other and I slowly said $300? She said okay if that was to take up and pull down. We agreed and quickly made more fliers targeting wealthy area grocery store parking lots.

I had a day job as a sales rep at the time as well. My brother took over most of the duties while I bought the lights in bulk. More than anything, the experience taught me to just try things. You never know who might like it. I also remember how many people were waiting to say it wouldn't work. I have had that experience in almost every venture I have ever started or been a part of.

People love to sit and be critics of those who strive to become more. My favorite quote is by Teddy Roosevelt:

> *It is not the critic who counts, not the man who points out how the strong man stumbles, or where the doer of deeds could have done them better. The credit belongs to the man who is actually in the arena, whose face is marred by dust and sweat and blood; who strives valiantly; who errs, who comes short again and again, because there is no effort without error and shortcoming; but who does actually strive to do the deeds; who knows great enthusiasms, the great devotions; who spends himself in a worthy cause; who at the best knows in the end the triumph of high achievement, and who at the worst, if he fails, at least fails while daring greatly, so that his place shall never be with those cold and timid souls who neither know victory nor defeat.*

> —Teddy Roosevelt in an excerpt from the speech "Citizenship in a Republic" delivered at the Sorbonne, in Paris, France on April 23, 1910

The first step in "becoming" something is to be brave. Be brave enough to realize that if you have your health, you should fear very little. Don't fear the critic or the naysayer; fear not trying; fear not finding the time. Not everything you try will work. And much of what you try will not fail. Just try!

Remember Tyler's bully story. Act or be acted upon. Same theme. Be the person on stage, not the masses watching.

Finding the Right Doctor

There is a point to my cancer story that goes beyond trying to make you feel sorry for me, which I hope you don't. It was a tremendous catalyst for me. But it also taught me an incredible lesson.

Some doctors really suck. In fact, in every industry there are people who are really good at their jobs and people that stink at them. I think until I had that experience it just never really occurred to me. You think that professionals like doctors, lawyers, pilots, etc., all have so much training they must be great at their jobs. Not the case. It turns out there are two main signs for testicular cancer. Can you guess what they are? A lump and chronic diarrhea. I told the general practitioner that when I was 17 years old. I had the tumor removed at 20. Weeks before seeing the urologist another doctor gave me antibiotics. Here is the thing. I am not mad that they did not know what was wrong with me. **What I am upset about is that they did not admit they did not know what was wrong with me.** Instead of sending me to a specialist, they either did nothing or *grossly* misdiagnosed the problem.

How often do we do this in life? How often do we seek help or advice from those who have zero experience in the subject? Or if they do have general experience, maybe it is not in the specific area we need help with. As I experienced, the potential problem with the generalist in giving advice, is they might not be honest about not knowing how to advise you.

Picking the right advisor (or doctor) is crucially important on the path of becoming.

In business I know many people: CEOs, CFOs, consultants, and the like. When Trace3 was growing at 100% year over year and everything was breaking, I turned to many of them for advice. Most gave it more than willingly. I had opinions flying at me from all directions. The problem is most advisors had never run a company that grew that fast.

Only one named Dave Hitz (founder of NetApp) had actually experienced that type of growth. He gave an amazing talk to the entire company about how everything was going to break almost every year…and that was to plan. Expect it. Thrive on it. If it is happening it means you are doing something most other companies could never accomplish. He implied that breaking your company's processes each year should be worn like a badge of honor. He turned it into a huge positive and set a baseline of a founder's mentality in the original Trace3 teams. We learned to expect and thrive in chaos.

Many of the others I spoke to focused on the negatives of fast growth and wanted to slow down in order to start operationalizing things. They wanted to look for ways to save money. Well, in a slower growth business, that may have made sense. I even tried some of it at times. It turns out, for what we were trying to do, it was the wrong advice. It was the wrong doctor for what ailed us. I needed to find a specialist, someone who had lived it and come out the other side. Hitz was that guy.

Later, when there was the mutiny and other chaos, I was not sure where to turn. As I said earlier, someone I respect handed me *The Advantage* by Patrick Lencioni and it completely changed everything. He and the Table Group were like corporate psychologists that came in and within two days had the leadership team understanding what ails us and were helping them address it.

I could go on with examples but I would instead encourage you to think of your history and think about advisors you have listened to in the past. When you have the right doctor, you almost always know it. It is the ones you are not sure about that usually end up screwing up. When you feel this way, keep looking.

Appetizers Before Entrees

When you are focused on "becoming," your first major hurdle is defining your *end state*. The end state is sort of like your finish line. I think the best end states are focused on value and not a monetary goal, but you can tie those two things together if you want. It should also be something that inspires you. If you have that end state in mind, you then need to do your best to make it tangible. Making it tangible involves building a breadcrumb-like plan that you can follow and hitting milestones along the way that eventually lead to the end state you are shooting for.

Let me give you an example of the wrong way to do this, then we can dissect it. When I originally came up with the idea for InstantScale (see Chapter 1), the end state was to slightly disintermediate venture investments by connecting startups directly to clients in order to build revenue via actual orders. We figured that cash coming in from orders was better than cash coming in from people requiring a piece of the entrepreneur's company. "Instantly scale" their revenue and put them in a more powerful position with the VCs and general market. For this service, we would ask for a small piece of equity in the company.

My original structure was for the startups to give me warrants based on our performance. If we could sell their product and drive up revenue (via Trace3), they would give us warrants. (Warrants are a form of equity.) We asked for far fewer warrants and less equity than a VC would and figured our end state goals would resonate with the entrepreneurs. I had great conversations with the CEOs of Riverbed, Palo Alto Networks, and Data Domain in their early stages. They all liked the concept, but really struggled with the equity structure since it was nontraditional. Jerry at Riverbed said no, but helped me write a term sheet for Frank at Data Domain. Data Domain liked it but when they found out Riverbed wasn't doing it, they also said no. Frank also let me know warrants were nontraditional and could have difficult tax treatments. Lane at Palo Alto had a few brief conversations with a couple board members about it and let me know no one liked the structure.

What I had done is gone out and led with my end state plan. I tried selling people on my end state for almost four years without convincing a single company to give me equity for the value prop. I have many examples in my career where I have screwed up like this.

Adriel Lares, one of my great friends and partners in Memento Mori, watched me bang my head against the wall with InstantScale the entire time. Finally I wised up and asked him for his thoughts. I had asked many others, but none of their advice seemed to work. I was almost ready to give up. As it turned out, the right doctor was at my fingertips the entire time. Adriel was a CFO of a public company and completely understood the difficulties around fundraising, boards, and equity structures much better than I ever would. He told me this, "Hayes, your value prop makes total sense. Everyone would rather give equity for money in the form of orders rather than give equity for just plan money. And having to give away less than half the equity for the order-based money is great too. Here is the problem. You are selling something no one has ever done before. You are offering a structure no one has ever done before. Instead of pitching the entrée, why don't you start with an appetizer? Give them something they know how to consume to start. Build credibility there. Then give them the next appetizer. Keep doing that until you have the credibility and references to serve up the entrée."

I said, "Ah...What?"

Adriel shook his head and laughed, "Just ask them if you can invest in the round. And for access into the funding round, you will prove the InstantScale value prop of getting them cash via orders from clients. Start with the traditional funding route. They find a lead VC firm to lead the round and you get to put in cash for a small piece of the round, therefore getting your equity and having a chance to prove what you can do."

Give them an appetizer. Make it easy for them to engage with you. Selling the end state is often just too hard for someone to swallow. The short version is after that conversation, InstantScale made 15 different investments over five years using Adriel's model instead of mine.

After we built some credibility over the first three years of investing and delivering on the InstantScale value prop, we've had four companies who let us invest and also gave us very small pieces of equity without us needing to give them money (my model).

"Appetizers before entrees". I owe Adriel many thanks for teaching me this lesson. I have applied it to so many things. It doesn't have to be starting a company. It works for hitting almost any type of goal.

Eating Your Babies

Point three in "being" versus "becoming" involves how comfortable you are with cannibalism.

I know it's a creepy metaphor, but the concept is simple and one that every one of us already intuitively understand.

Why did Blackberry struggle to make a smartphone? What happened to Nokia? Blockbuster watched Netflix for years and did nothing. Where is Kodak today? Do you remember the computer companies Gateway, DEC, SGI, or Sun Microsystems? Do you remember when Barnes & Noble and Amazon used to do the same basic thing? Why did HP and Symantec each split into two companies?

Some of these names were (are) great companies. The people running these companies and sitting on the boards were incredibly smart. At a given moment in time, all were innovators. Arguably, they were some of the best innovators out there. These innovations that they brought to market were almost like their babies. They were the founding reasons for their success in the market. They birthed them and were watching them grow and mature over the years.

Psychologically, it is pretty easy to take risk when you have nothing. If you have nothing to lose, taking chances even seems like the right move because if you fail it will be a pretty short fall. There are also very limited expectations on you when you have little. The opposite is also true. When you have birthed something special into the market and possibly created an entirely new space with companies chasing you, you have something to lose.

When you create something of value and that value is recognized, even the best of the best have a tendency to protect it. "Becoming" is hard! They did it successfully. They birthed an innovation, took it to market, created massive wealth, and now have turf to protect! They already "became" something. So the tendency is to stop becoming and switch to being. When this happens, your enterprise risks becoming obsolete. This is why it is so important to be looking at the "home runs" set both personally and companywide on a regular basis. It can help give perspective on whether you are becoming stagnant.

It is not always the leaders in these companies who fail. In many cases, they recognize the need to change. The recognize that they need to strive to innovate more even if that means eating their babies they so dearly love. Where many of them failed was to get the rest of the company to recognize it. Deep down, no one wants to cannibalize their creation. It can feel like cutting off your own arm. So instead they try to improve the baby. They can evolve it so it can compete with the new threats in the market. They convince management that a new product or offering might be too hard to make or cost too many people their jobs. In some of the companies listed in this chapter, not eating their babies cost every single person their job.

The take-away here is that when you get to the point that you have something to lose, keep your eyes open. Realize that protecting what you have created, or your personal skillset, or a relationship, is not about putting it in a box so no one can hurt it. It is about being willing to evolve it to keep it valuable and ahead of the curve. If you are unlucky enough to have someone who has absolutely nothing to lose enter your market with a true innovation or offering to threaten your baby, you are going to *have* to act. Sitting their just "being" could be a death sentence. Figure out how to segment who is with you in becoming competitive and who is going to roadblock and just be.

Lead from the Front

The last point is that you can't delegate "becoming" to someone else. It can absolutely be done with a team or group, but you need to step up and lead from the front. You need to be in the trenches willing to share the risk with the front lines.

When I think about this, I always get the visual of that one scene in the movie *Braveheart* where Mel Gibson's character is on the hill with all his troops who are out numbered and out trained by the opposing forces. He gives them a talk about what is at stake...about why they are fighting and why the cause is so important. Then instead of sending them on in front of him, he leads the charge. The emotional reaction when your leader you believe in jumps into the fray is to double your level of effort. We just don't want to let leaders like that down. We want to fight next to them and we want to protect them and their ideals.

Change is hard. I have a hard time thinking of an example where someone or something goes from just being something to becoming something and it does not involve change and tough choices.

Those We Serve

I would like to present you with one last use-case that encompasses much of what has been covered in previous chapters. It is not a corporate use-case. It is based around helping others. It is around lifting up those who need a hand out of a bad situation.

Who Are You Serving and How Real Is the Value You Provide?

This is always a good question to ask with any new project/venture. Thinking and writing about this will help to center your thoughts as you begin. Who is it you are trying to serve?

What follows is the story of a charity that I participated in as it traveled through the concepts covered in the book. The story is real and may be one of the things I am most proud to have been a part of.

> I joined the board of a charity called Project Hope Alliance (PHA) many years ago. PHA was in the business of helping homeless kids get an education. When I joined they had vans that picked up kids from motels, shelters, etc., and drove them to a specific school. The vans went far and wide to get the kids. The foundation funded the transportation and some services the school provided.

> At the end of the school day, we shuttled these grade K-8 kids back to motels, shelters, etc., where there was nowhere to do homework, cook, wash clothes, sleep, or truly even think about much of anything but their predicament.

> Was shuttling them providing real meaningful value? Yes, but it not enough.

© Hayes Drumwright 2017
H. Drumwright, *Management vs. Employees*, DOI 10.1007/978-1-4842-1675-0_12

Think about your "they" and be honest with yourself. Are you providing real value to those you serve? Is the value transformational? Could it be?

Figure Out What You Are Dealing With

If your value falls short, where do you turn? The answer is to find a simple way to do discovery. Your goal in discovery is simple and quick, not perfect.

> *At Project Hope, we wanted to help the kids and had many arguments about how possible that would be without taking into account their pre- and post-school environments. We starting looking at the parent's situations. Many had jobs. A good portion of our kid's families had lost homes and cars in the housing crisis. They could pay rents and car payments, but their credit was shot and they did not have money for first and last month rent and security deposits.*

> *We came up with a theory that if we could help the families gain sustainable stable living options, our chances to provide real value to the children would skyrocket.*

Include Many in the Solving and Focus on Those You Serve

You have examined critically the value you are providing and have also done discovery around what real value will look like to those you serve. The next step is figuring out how to solve for it and start executing.

> *In the process of discovery, I got worried because I did not know how to solve what we had discovered. During that time, PHA was able to recruit a board member named Jennifer Friend. She was a partner at a law firm with a great career and amazing family. Jennifer had deep knowledge on what our families were going through. She revealed to the board that she grew up moving from motel to motel and hiding it from friends and schoolmates.*

> *To further our efforts and solve for our roadblocks, she recruited 3-4 others to the board who had deep knowledge and deep pockets. We then reached out to other foundations running shelters and programs helping homeless families to learn what had worked and failed for them.*

> *During this time, most all the board members who were there when I originally joined resigned. That was hard. But I knew that could happen as we reached for transformational value.*

I kept my "they" (the kids we were trying to help) at the front of my decision-making process when times were hard. Even as the Executive Director (a great lady) decided she would step down, we pushed forward knowing how important what we were trying to do was. Jennifer, after including many in the solving process, laid out a plan showing how PHA could move families into permanent housing for under $2,000 per family. We built a board with different types to people to accomplish Jennifer's plan and we were able to convince her to champion the cause (that she helped develop). She left her law firm and became the CEO of PHA.

A key takeaway is this step can be hard. There will be conflict. Watch out for attribution error and don't make the conflict personal. Any argument must be grounded in increasing the value for those you serve to stay healthy.

Never Stop Improving

Your first plans can almost never be perfect. What you initially thought was super valuable to your audience might change as you get deeper into it. There is also a chance that as you provide them value, secondary needs arise that you will need to pay attention to. Keep looking for value, getting many involved in solving for it, and never stop trying to improve.

In the first year, Jennifer and the PHA team ended the cycle of homelessness for over 70 kids. She iterated on the "Family Assistance Program" by looking at national programs and the data she received from the families she served. She was asked to join national teams and speak at more and more events as her success rates improved.

To date, Jennifer has led the charge and ended the cycle of homelessness for over 800 children and their parents in just three years.

Funding is up over 500% and the service levels that PHA provides for the children has consistently grown. At this point, many want her to take her program and methodology national.

Success breeds success if you continue to look for true value and iterate. Be willing to experiment and know failure will occur. Pivot out of it and move to a new experiment.

A Legacy of Failure

I read *David and Goliath* by Malcolm Gladwell a little while ago. There were many stories in that book I found fascinating. But even years later one of the discussions that really stuck with me was how first generation immigrants worked so incredibly hard and what a difficult time they had transferring that work ethic onto the next generation. Why is that? Why is one generation so focused on "becoming" something, often to make sure their children have a better life than they did, while the next is often comfortable just "being"? (There is a great deal more to it and I would encourage you to read the book.)

The book makes you think that our advantages might actually be disadvantages for the next generation. That maybe hardship and what are normally perceived as negative things like dyslexia or other ailments might actually make us stronger. The need to overcome might just source from the fact that you had no choice but to overcome. You arrive in a new land with nothing; you can't read or comprehend simple words, so you must develop a work-around. Gladwell even talks about how losing a parent at an early age can set children on a path for overachieving. Fascinating.

Well, regardless of what you think about Gladwell, he does have a tendency to make you think. It worked on me. I in no way had what most would consider a tough upbringing but it was not always smooth sailing either. As I grew up, my family lost everything a couple times and struggled to rebuild financial

© Hayes Drumwright 2017
H. Drumwright, *Management vs. Employees*, DOI 10.1007/978-1-4842-1675-0_13

freedom. According to Gladwell, I was probably very lucky to experience the financial rise and fall. There is something to learn at the peaks and valleys. In fact, one could argue that a constant peak without a valley teaches you almost nothing of value. It might possibly even prescribe all the wrong things.

Success is a lousy teacher. It seduces smart people into thinking they can't lose.

—Bill Gates

Kids Shouldn't Be Your Legacy

It was with this thought in mind that I started to devise a plan. I think when many of us think about our legacy, we often think of our children. I don't know if I am a bit dense or not, but I have never liked that thought. I have four children. Three boys and the youngest is a girl. As will be the case with most all parents, my children's safety, happiness, and future are incredibly important to me. But for me, the kids are not my legacy. I believe that puts far too much pressure on them to fit into a mold I might make for them. I want them to have a certain sureness in their hearts: that I believe in them, that anything is possible with effort, that working smart is better than just working hard, that how they act is more important than what they say, and that beauty comes from kindness and good looks can be derived from intelligence. I could go on with these different principles but I won't. I love my kids and I want them to have a terrific foundation to battle in this world. But they are not my legacy. My hope is they will create their own legacies and I intend to be cheering from the sidelines as long as I can.

At some point, I decided I would stop talking about my successes too much in front of them.

I remember a simple version of this that my dad did with me. He swam on a scholarship at a university. I swam in college as well. I would always ask him about his times. We did not swim the same event, as he was a freestyle sprinter and I was a backstroker, but he never would tell me his times. He would just say that he couldn't really remember. I am not sure why I let that slide because swimmers always know their times down to the tenth of a second; but I did. I found out years later he was incredibly fast. Much faster than I had ever been. I never felt compared to him or like I was chasing him or his times. I was racing myself and constantly trying to improve. And he was always there to cheer.

Show Your Struggle

As I write this, my oldest son is 11 and my daughter is 3. I stepped down from Trace3 as CEO approximately two years ago. I decided over a year ago that I would only talk to my kids about POPin and not the success of Trace3.

My kids had missed my many impressive "ball-of-flame" company disasters. They missed the time I tried to buy out another company by joining as an employee and having half my commissions go into an escrow account until it hit a watermark. When the watermark was achieved ownership would be turned over to me. Total failure on that one… They missed the fundraising company for schools where my partner very cleverly siphoned the money out via a marketing company his friend owned. That one didn't even make it two years.

They missed the first year of Memento Mori where we were worried the 13 barrels of wine we had waited on for two years to age would not be good enough for the blend. We thought there was a 50/50 chance we would have to write off the whole vintage. Luckily we blended the five best barrels and had an amazing inaugural vintage. They missed the constant nerves and stress of starting Trace3 with no money.

Basically, all my kids knew of me and work was that we were safe, secure, and didn't need to worry about much. So I came home from work one day and changed the conversation:

> We went through the normal routine of asking everyone the highs and lows of their days. When it got around to me, my oldest asked how my day was. I said this, "Well…I am a little worried." This was not normal so suddenly everyone was paying attention. "I left my safe job at Trace3 to take a big risk on this new idea I had. I used a bunch of my own money to start POP and the entire time I have worked there I have not taken a paycheck."

> "Why?" said my eight year old.

> "When you work for a startup company sometimes they do not have enough money to pay you. I am trying to use all the money I can in POP to get the right people on board to make it a success. And it started out really good. We got a bunch of clients right when we started, but growing the business so I can make a paycheck is taking longer than I had hoped. It is harder than I thought. I think I am going to have to go and raise money from people called venture capitalist…I have never done that before and to be honest it makes me a little scared."

Now mind you, everything I said was true. Completely true. My experiences raising money at Techfuel (my 1997-2000 failure) had totally scarred me. I had pulled together most every smart person (doctor) I knew who had success-fully raised money and asked them for advice. My network in Silicon Valley was strong. I knew many of the VCs at this point in my career and with the help of my successful peers had set over 20 meetings with top tier firms.

> *"I am going to be traveling to Northern California a lot in the next 3-4 weeks and I hope that one of the companies I talk to will decide to give POP funding. If they do, we would be set up for the next 18 months to try and make something I believe in very much."*

> *"Daddy," said my six year old, "What if they don't give you the money?"*

> *"Well, I would be in some trouble then. We would not have enough money to keep POP alive and I might have to shut down the company. Not just Daddy, but everyone at POP would lose their jobs."*

The conversation continued to talk of money saved, could we lose the house, and should they start to lemonade stands to help save money just in case. While the last thought was thrown on the table by my youngest son, I saw something change in the oldest's eyes. I think a change for the better.

After my first trip up north all the kids wanted to know was how the fundrais-ing went. Same with the employees of POP for that matter. I told everyone at POP that the fundraising would be something I would have to shoulder. As I learned where the truth in value was from Silicon Valley's perspective, I would pass it on to the team and they could use it to continue making the product and client base more impressive. That was truly the best way they could con-tribute to the cause. I could not promise how fast we could get the funding but if every time I traveled to Silicon Valley I had new things to show the VCs, we would have a better chance of success. They couldn't be there with me, but they could definitely help. The team put their heads down and worked incredibly hard.

> *Upon returning from my first trip, I told the family I had failed. I met with five firms and all had said no. This includes the one I had the best relationship with. The boys looked a little shocked. One asked if we would lose the house. We used this again as a way to talk about how loans and expenses work and how if you are smart you can try to manage them down in good times for experiences just like this. I told them I thought we were okay for now, but the failure really hurt because some of the people I met with were my friends and I thought they would fund me.*

> *I told them my plan did not work; I was worried, and a little sad. I asked them what they thought I should do.*

My oldest looked at me and said, "You can't quit Dad. Drumwrights don't quit." The other two followed his lead. My wife who was always there taking care of all of us bent her head a bit so her hair was in her face and I saw the hint of a proud smile. I felt my eyes begin to water a little.

It was incredibly freeing to be so honest. To let them see my concern and worry. To let them see that life could be lived without a backstop and have failure lurking around every corner.

This went on from July to October. I received over 20 negative responses. I was truly concerned. Every week the conversation at the table got a bit more dire. We started discussing backup plans if the funding didn't work. When we went out to dinner or talked about small trips, the older two wanted to know if we had enough money to be doing them. I told them, while work was hard and things were not going super well I would not over extend us with dinners and small trips. This gave us a chance to talk about savings, credit cards, and budgets.

We talked about all these important things in a way that they wanted to hear it and cared about because they were now a bit invested. They cared because they had a voice and were allowed to be concerned right along with me. I think they trusted we would be okay, but they had a healthy concern. As an example, I specifically remember my 11 year old being offered a chance to go and play soccer in France for a week with some boys on his club team and sitting me down to ask if that would cost the family too much money. I was floored at the change.

In early October, when POP received a term sheet for $6M, we had quite a celebration at home. The hugs and joy in their eyes was pretty awesome. I let them know how much their support really mattered and bolstered my spirits when I was down. I told them that when they had a time like this in their lives not to walk it alone. Have a support system. And for sure...call me and I would repay the favor.

Weeks later, I tried showing the hiring plan to my oldest but could see it went over his head. I may try again at some point, but we do talk about burn rates sometimes. We talk about trying to weigh the risks of going fast into the unknown versus waiting to see what happens. We talk about acting versus being acted upon.

As I look back on those four months, I think my favorite memories will be talking about how I failed and that failing was a normal part of growing. It spawned pretty amazing conversations. I still have to remind myself from time to time not to talk or brag about successes with them. I let them see when I am excited when good things happen, but sharing the failures is where the magic happens. Life and business is not easy and they should know that. It is not my job to block that from them but to arm them for their futures. I really do believe in sharing a healthy amount of risk or or else suffer feelings of entitlement.

A Hero's Story

As a general rule of leadership, I believe we should all talk more about our failures than our successes. It humanizes us. It draws people in. And how great is that since some of our best teaching moments are not in how we succeeded but in why we failed.

Tyler, the author of the bully story and CEO of Trace3, once broke down for me the "hero's" journey that we see in books and the movies all the time and I think it applies here. I was fascinated when I was listening to him and realized I had not really dissected it before. There are really deep versions of this dissection online but here is the way Tyler described it to me:

- The hero comes from humble beginnings.

- The hero finds a cause worth fighting for.

- The hero finds a mentor and, in training and fighting for the cause, builds a small following.

- The hero steps out of the mentor's shadow and it is hard to say at this point if the followers believe more in the cause or the hero…

- There are setbacks (sometimes huge ones) and the hero, instead of giving up like most of us would, steps forward and personally leads the group (or does it alone) to overcome them.

- The followers, inspired by the hero, start to raise the cause above themselves or the hero and fight on their own.

- The hero has now created many new heroes via this journey and now even if he dies, the cycle can repeat into sequels if not trilogies.

William Wallace screaming "freedom" as he dies. Jerry Maguire says, "Help me help you". *Field of Dreams*—If you build it they will come. *Hunger Games* to the Mockingjay. *Guardians of the Galaxy* join forces to destroy some big creepy dude. You get the point. But there is something to take seriously in this formula. It is a formula of the underdog and it is inspiring. We want the underdog to triumph. We cheer for them and relate to them.

Think about the four months with my boys. The struggle was mine. Then it became ours. I was humble and vulnerable, admitting I might not be able to pull it off. But I would not quit. The company worked and worked and by October had built something that could overcome the "no's" and turn them into a yes. I so hope…so hope, that I have four little heroes in the making. Four heroes that by watching me fail, strive, fail again, yet continues to strive eventually find causes and a legacy of their own.

A "hero's" passion for the cause will slowly infect others. That really is the kind of connection we want to build with the ones we serve. In my travels in my career, I decided I needed to build a platform to make that happen via POPin. Whether you leverage it or take another route is not as important as realizing you need a route to create your own legacy. Identify the "they" you want to serve, build a cause around them, connect to them, attract like-minded followers, and don't quit. Failure is a way to learn. Wear it like a badge of honor. Don't keep failing at the same things over and over, but use failure as a way to teach and learn will only gather new followers (potential heroes).

I don't think any of us expect the journey to be easy. Being versus becoming is hard whether with a company or on a personal level. Sometimes reaching our legacy can just be about ourselves and our personal accomplishments. I have friends that have done full Ironman triathlons or climbed insane mountains. Some have been professional athletes or actors. I don't want to discount any of this because a legacy that only involves one person can be powerful and important. It can be something for others to admire and chase.

For me, a legacy is about more than just self. It has very little to do with the hero and almost everything to do with others. Please don't confuse this type of legacy as someone who is a saint who is never out for personal gain, because it does not have to be that way. I don't think creating a rich legacy and creating personal wealth (or quality of life) have to be mutually exclusive. One can lead to the other and possibly even be a catalyst for the other. Regardless, a legacy focused on lifting, healing, or creating a future for others is inspiring to many of us. The simplest example would be charity work. Extreme examples include people like Elon Musk, who has a goal of colonizing Mars, or someone like Jonas Salk, who developed a vaccine for Polio.

In the end, I think we all want our lives to matter in some way and having a tangible legacy is something many of us aspire to. My hope is that, as you have been reading between the lines in this book, you have seen a bit of a blueprint for creating a legacy based on the concepts covered in the book.

Chapter 1: In setting goals or starting ventures, who are the ones you are trying to provide value for and why?

Chapter 2: What does your ego, a solid foundation, and learning from failure have to do with creating opportunity?

Chapter 3: Your superpower is to admit you screwed up and that you are willing to keep screwing up.

Chapter 4: How do you deal with entitlement and apathy in a way that lets them know you really care?

Chapter 5: Our background can jade our perception of others, lead to unhealthy conflict, and cause waste at a frightening pace.

Chapter 6: In organizations most all communication goes one way and doesn't work. Doing more of it, louder each time, won't fix it.

Chapter 7: Build a bridge by letting them speak up specifically about something that matters to them. Help with their problems to build trust.

Chapter 8: Find a way for them to tell you the truth in a way you can make some sense out of it. Goodwill, while easier in the moment, is a legacy killer.

Chapter 9: Go lean to start. Then test and iterate by leveraging a platform that provides safety for the truth and allows for healthy conflict to increase engagement and buy-in from the stakeholders. Spend as you go, not all upfront.

Chapter 10: How can you drive adoption from groups outside of the company?

Chapter 11: Use the right mentors, take small steps, stay vigilant, and step to the front.

Chapter 12: With something already up and running, how do you examine whether you are delivering real value? Source, solve, and iterate works regardless of the vertical.

If you are thinking, "Crap! Why did I read this whole book if he was just going to list the cliff notes in Chapter 13?" I feel for you, but know I did tell the publisher to use a big font and small pages so it was easier to read. I tried to tell stories and use tangible examples all throughout the book mainly for the purpose of trying to create this blueprint of creating a legacy.

I did this because you are my "they" for this book! *I am writing this book to try to help people Act instead of Be Acted Upon. I created POPin for the same reason.* Real leadership is hard work. It is a decision and quite honestly is it never really "required." Deciding to do it and take it seriously is never the homework; it is always extra credit.

What are your ventures? Could you write a chapter and describe them and how you serve them? I think if you can, you can begin to see your legacy on the horizon. Not all of us can colonize Mars but if purposefully built, the combination of ventures you pursue in life can begin to build a narrative for your legacy.

Where to Start

I was recently listening to a speaker who brought me out of my normal daydreaming and caused me to pay attention. He threw out two questions:

1. Do we all need a boss?

2. Who/what gives you rules?

Initially my answer was "no" to the first question. I mean I have been running companies for quite a while now and would consider myself a self-starter who does not rely on having a direct boss for direction. So logically, if my answer is "no" to question number 1 you would think that the answer to question 2 is pretty straightforward. If I don't need a boss then you would assume I am the master of my own destiny and I give myself all the rules. Unfortunately, that answer for question 2 felt pretty hollow.

Do you need a boss and who gives you rules to operate from? As I normally do, I started to consider the questions in terms of my family versus my work. With my kids, I would say they definitely need a boss. Left to depend on themselves and their innate nature, I would guess they might not be able to take care of themselves quite yet. Kids need parents to teach them how to stay safe and give them an approach to tackle the world. By themselves, they would be in trouble and have too steep a learning curve.

Luckily for most parents there comes an inflection point where slowly the kids start to take on more and more responsibility and leave the nest as "adults." Now, when these young adults have left the nest, how would they answer question 2? It is probably the question that keeps parents up at night the most. Your kids have gone and who is giving them the rules now? We hope the moral code they learned growing up serves as guideposts in decision making, but we know there will be situations they will encounter out in the great wide world that we have not (and could not) have prepared them for. Let's transition from talking about young adults and talk about our personal situations.

I was talking with my friend Adriel about the questions and asked him how he would answer. His answer to number 2 stopped me in my tracks. He said the "path" we choose gives us our rules.

The path we choose will create options, opportunity, danger, and problems for us as we try to reach a destination. When you start a business, enter a marriage, have children, start a new job, buy a house, or make any major life decisions, you are choosing a path. In many cases, the path you choose will dictate much of the playing field.

Is that where you stop? The path you choose dictates the rules and you operate within them? Does that fundamentally agree with you?

How hard is it for a person to have a boss (read "parent") most all of their younger years and then finally graduate out on their own just to start a job under a new boss? Didn't they just spend most of their life proving they were worthy of being treated like an adult? Bummer, huh? These are the internal battles I have fought for years that made me want to start writing this book.

I believe people want to be treated like adults. I don't just believe it; I think in business it is a fact.

At the same time, I think most of us if left to our own devices are inherently flawed in many ways. All of us have at one time or another acted in a way where someone should have revoked our "adult" cards.

So we want and feel we deserve to be treated like adults, but know we are flawed and screw up a lot. Troubling. This is the reason the "them" section of this book exists. Whether you are an imperfect leader or an imperfect person being led, the psychology matters and needs to be considered when choosing your path.

Choosing a job is choosing a company. It is also choosing a path. That path will most likely have a boss. To hold our excitement, we need to believe in the cause of the company and feel the boss (and the rules) has our future interests at heart. A best case would be where the leader judged her success as a representation of the success of the team and would be inclusive. We would want clarity of purpose and to be given say on how we could accomplish it. We would want shared accountability and the freedom to experiment and make mistakes. If we could find all those things, then we have to do our part and serve those as best we can in a way that moves everyone forward. We must put aside apathy and entitlement, recognize personal and corporate attribution error, and be extremely honest when asked to contribute.

"They Come First" has provided a path to accomplish these things. It is a path that leads somewhere valuable. It is a path that starts with selflessness and ends with tremendous personal reward. This is especially true if personal reward was never the goal.

I

Index

© Hayes Drumwright 2017
H. Drumwright, *Management vs. Employees*, DOI 10.1007/978-1-4842-1675-0

Get the eBook for only $5!

Why limit yourself?

Now you can take the weightless companion with you wherever you go and access your content on your PC, phone, tablet, or reader.

Since you've purchased this print book, we're happy to offer you the eBook in all 3 formats for just $5.

Convenient and fully searchable, the PDF version enables you to easily find and copy code—or perform examples by quickly toggling between instructions and applications. The MOBI format is ideal for your Kindle, while the ePUB can be utilized on a variety of mobile devices.

To learn more, go to www.apress.com/companion or contact support@apress.com.

Made in the USA
Middletown, DE
11 September 2016